BY YANG JWING-MING

SHAOLIN
CHIN NA

THE SEIZING ART OF KUNG-FU

UNIQUE
PUBLICATIONS

© **UNIQUE PUBLICATIONS, INC., 1982**
All rights reserved
Printed in the United States of America
ISBN: 0-86568-012-4
Library of Congress No.: 80-53546

DISCLAIMER

To Master Li Mao Ching and Master Cheng Gin Gsao.

ACKNOWLEDGEMENTS

The author wishes to thank Vidas Gvozdzius, Jeff Bolt, Cosmin Theodore, Rod Engle, and Lee Burneson for their help with this book.

Table of Contents

PREFACE

This book, which is solely devoted to Chin Na, was written for a variety of reasons. But before going into those reasons, it would be helpful if the reader first had an idea about the nature and purpose of Chin Na. Chin Na are special grappling and pressing techniques whose basic purpose is to control a person. Although many Chin Na techniques are designed to control without killing, there are techniques which are meant to "control" a person by death. The techniques themselves involve controlling a person by grasping, twisting, bending, or occasionally striking nerves (cavities), muscles, and joints. Chin Na techniques exist at two levels: fundamental and advanced. The fundamental techniques involve simple external power, little knowledge of Chin Na theory, and a small acquaintance with human anatomy. The advanced techniques, on the other hand, involve internal power, external penetrating power, a complete understanding of Chin Na theory, and an intimate knowledge of human anatomy. The art of Chin Na obviously includes more than mere formula and technique; it also involves aspects from traditional Chinese medicine.

Returning to the motivations for writing this book, the first reason is for the sake of the knowledge itself. If any aspect of Kung Fu, and even Wu Su as a whole, is to survive in our modern society, where career and business concerns take precedence, then Kung Fu must not be a secret art. If Chinese martial artists can show the best of their styles and knowledge, and if people can see through the mystification that others with little knowledge propagate, then Kung Fu will be seen as a living art which is worth preserving.

The second reason for writing this book is that no current edition written in English exists with Chin Na as its main subject. Most books on martial arts give little or no space to Chin Na. This book, therefore, aims to show Chin Na techniques, theory, and training methods as they are particularly found in Eagle Claw, White Crane, and Long Fist. By presenting the Chin Na from these styles, the reader will have a more than adequate understanding of it. This understanding will come about because Eagle Claw and White Crane have made Chin Na into highly developed specialties; their systems are among the most comprehensive within Chinese Wu Su.

Eagle Claw and White Crane in themselves are complementary systems which, if taken together, involve almost all the types of Chin Na. For instance, Eagle Claw emphasizes *misplacing the bone, dividing the muscle,* and *sealing the breath or vein* Chin Na, while White Crane emphasizes *cavity press* and *grasping the muscle* Chin Na; these types comprise every category of Chin Na. (Refer to Chapter 2 for an explanation of these types.) This book, then, will present the best of both systems.

Although Chin Na techniques are important, Chin Na has traditionally been only a small, yet important, part of any style. Every Chinese Wu Su style will have a number of Chin Na techniques (many of them the same), but Chin Na by itself is never the *major* emphasis or specialty. In Chinese Wu Su there is no traditional Chin Na division.

An additional feature of this book is the ease by which a martial artist can learn Chin Na. In many instances, the mastery of technical matter involves some previous experience or the help of an instructor; but given the nature of most Chin Na techniques, they can be easily learned from a book giving adequate directions and photographs. For martial artists practicing a style with little or no Chin Na, this book can give them a valuable number of extra techniques. Although not every technique can be easily mastered, most can be learned if the martial artist constantly practices them.

Turning now to the contents of this volume, the first chapter will be a general introduction. This chapter will focus on the history of Chin Na, especially through the Eagle Claw and White Crane divisions. These histories are important since most of the Chin Na are taken from those divisions. This chapter will also include a special section on the founder of Eagle Claw, Marshal Yeuh Fei.

The second chapter will deal with the theory and types of Chin Na. The types to be explained will be dividing the muscle, misplacing the bone, sealing the breath or vein, and cavity press. By understanding how a Chin Na technique works, the martial artist can learn and apply the forms more easily. By having this theoretical basis, the martial artist can judge for himself the usefulness of certain Chin Na techniques.

The third chapter will contain fundamental training and knowledge. In order to effectively apply Chin Na, the martial artist must train himself in certain ways. The chapter will especially focus on fundamental stances, hand forms, and power and speed training. Before anybody can attempt to apply the Chin Na techniques in free fighting, he must have a solid grounding in fundamentals; otherwise, the Chin Na techniques can hurt more than help.

The fourth chapter on massage is an important and unique chapter. The theory behind it is important for understanding the basis of fundamental and advanced Chin Na; both massage and advanced Chin Na use and recognize the concept of a cavity. The concept of a cavity is also important in understanding Chi and Chi circulation. As this chapter will reveal, Chinese Wu Su has used and contributed to many aspects of traditional Chinese medicine, especially acupressure.

The actual fundamental and advanced techniques will be shown in Chapter 5. The fundamental techniques will only contain dividing the muscle and misplacing the bone. The advanced techniques will focus mainly on sealing the breath or vein and cavity press. In addition, the theory and methods of healing injuries which result from the practice and application of both fundamental and advanced Chin Na will be discussed.

In Chapter 6 the practical applications of Chin Na will be discussed. While Chapter 5 contains the basic formulas for Chin Na, Chapter 6 will show how to use these Chin Na in free fighting and knife or dagger struggles.

The author hopes this book will offer to the practicing martial artist and martial scholar a comprehensive discussion of an important part of Chinese Wu Su. By constant practice, the martial artist can find Chin Na to be a useful tool in short and middle range fighting. I hope that this book can act as a guide for other martial artists to begin open discussion on the special strengths and techniques of their styles with other practitioners. Such an effort can only help martial arts.

CHAPTER 1

GENERAL INTRODUCTION

Definition of Kung Fu

In discussing any aspect of Chinese martial arts, such as Chin Na, it would be helpful to have a general introduction to Kung Fu. Kung Fu, in the Chinese language, means "energy" (*kung*) and "time" (*fu*). Together both words mean a kind of patient accomplishment. To master any skill naturally requires patience or energy and time; this term can be applied to nonmartial skills such as music and art. When a person has mastered his particular skill, he may be said to have kung fu. The term became associated with martial arts because the mastery of any martial system required, and still requires, years of dedicated practice. But in everyday usage, the common term for martial arts is *Wu Su* or "martial technique." Sometimes the term *Wu Kung* is used for martial arts—this word translates as "martial Kung Fu."

Another important word which is used for martial arts is *Kuo Su* which translates as "national technique." In 1928 this word was coined by the Nationalist government in China when the Nan King Central Kuo Su Institute was created for the purpose of rebuilding Wu Su. Many Chinese martial artists currently use this word.

Kung Fu as a whole has been traditionally divided into two groups of categories. The first category of Northern and Southern is based on a geographical division while the second category of external and internal is based on differences in approach to certain features of martial training. These terms will be mentioned later in this chapter.

Introduction to Chin Na

In the Chinese language Chin Na roughly translates into two words: "seize" (*chin,*) and "control" (*na*). From this definition, the implication is that the major purpose of Chin Na is to quiet or stop an aggressive action without maiming or injuring to a serious extent. As a result, Chin Na mainly relies on grasping, pressing, and unnaturally twisting the sensitive parts of an opponent's body such as nerves, muscles, and joints. Chin Na does include a certain number of strikes, but these are usually aimed at spots which will cause an opponent momentary paralysis or unconsciousness. Although the primary purpose of Chin Na is control, there are some Chin Na techniques which are used to kill or maim.

In all, there are four types of Chin Na: "dividing the muscle" (*Fen Gin*); "misplacing the bone" (*Tsuoh Guu*); "sealing the breath or vein" (*Bih Chi, Duann Mie*); and "cavity press" (*Tien Hsueh*); the first two are fundamental and the others are advanced. The first two Chin Na control a person by attacking muscles and joints; these types usually involve some type of bending, twisting, or grasping. Sealing the breath or vein basically involves cutting off the supply of oxygen to the brain or lung. Cavity press Chin Na involves attacking, by the use of internal power or external penetration power, certain points on the nerves called cavities. When certain cavities are pressed with enough power, momentary paralysis, fainting, or death by internal organ failure can result. The location of many cavities are usually well kept secrets within any style. The advanced techniques, compared to the fundamental, require much more knowledge in such areas as anatomy and Chi cycles (see Chapter 4).

In Chinese Wu Su, Chin Na techniques are more or less learned and researched by every style. Among the Southern styles, which specialize in hand techniques and in short and middle range fighting, White Crane has one of the more complete systems of Chin Na. Another Southern style which puts heavy emphasis on Chin Na is Tiger Claw. Among the Northern styles, which specialize in kicking and long and middle range fighting, Eagle Claw places heavy emphasis on Chin Na. Long Fist, which uses the Eagle Claw system, is another Northern style with many Chin Na techniques.

Although Chin Na is intimately connected with Chinese Wu Su, a person does not need to have extensive martial experience to learn Chin Na. Chin Na techniques are basically independent of any martial style and can be learned by anyone willing to devote time and energy. Currently, some Chin Na techniques are being used by policemen with no formal background in martial arts to help them control a person without having to use a gun.

Because this book shows the Chin Na taken from the Eagle Claw, Long Fist, and White Crane styles, it is important to get an idea of their histories and relationship to the author's training. Chin Na techniques have a long history and have been involved with many famous martial artists. With a historical perspective the reader gains an extra understanding of Chin Na and Kung Fu in general.

Chin Na History

The Eagle Claw (*Yeuh Jar Ien Jao*) was founded by General Yeuh Fei during the Sung dynasty around 1130 A.D. in Huo Pei province. Although General Yeuh created the principles which distinguish Eagle Claw, his style like many others had it's foundation in the system taught by the Shao Lin Temple.

Before 527 A.D., the Shao Lin Temple existed as a Buddhist monastery where worshipping and religious teaching was done. But in 527 A.D. the Shao Lin Temple made the first step toward including martial arts as a course of study. That year an Indian Buddhist Prince named Da Mo (fig. 1) arrived at the temple to preach. While preaching he noticed that the monks were very weak; as a result, he decided to help them. Da Mo then locked himself in a room for nine years of meditation to find a way of helping the monks. When he came out he wrote down his results in two books: *Shi Sui Ching* and *Yi Gin Ching*. The *Shi Sui Ching* was primarily a religious treatise explaining methods for developing the Buddhist spirit while the *Yi Gin Ching* taught ways to strengthen the physical body. The *Yi Gin Ching* was taught for generations in the Shao Lin Temple to increase the health and strength of the monks.

The monks started practicing Da Mo's methods and soon found that they had gained enormously in strength. After this the monks began developing martial forms to complement their power. This process was kept up for hundreds of years until the Shao Lin system became the greatest martial art organization in China. Even after the Shao Lin system became the greatest in China, it still kept improving for hundreds of years.

In the tenth century the Shao Lin Temple had established a few more temples in various places around China. The temples which existed taught external Wu Su and internal Wu Su; usually one system was taught and emphasized before the other. One temple which practiced internal Wu Su before external Wu Su was located on Wu Dan Mountain in Fu Bei province. Roughly, the external style emphasized perfecting technique before developing internal power; likewise, the internal style emphasized building up internal power before the perfecting of external technique. The internal system of the Shao Lin Temple was the forerunner of present day internal styles like Tai Chi and Ba Kua.

Seven hundred years after Da Mo first arrived at the Shao Lin Temple, Eagle Claw was created by Yeuh Fei during the Sung dynasty (960–1279 A.D.). Yeuh Fei at that time began to teach his soldiers two systems of martial arts, using as a foundation the Shao Lin style that was taught to him by Chou Ton; Chou Ton learned his martial arts directly from the Shao Lin Temple. The first martial art that Yeuh Fei taught was from the internal style and based on Da Mo's *Yi Gin Ching*. This system is the parent of the present day style of Hsing I.

But more important for this story, General Yeuh Fei used his external Shao Lin foundation to create the style of Eagle Claw. Yeuh's Eagle Claw gave a special place to Chin Na within the style. The success of Yeuh's Eagle Claw–trained troops soon made the new style a well known and respected division.

At this point, it is necessary to introduce the concept of key words. Every complete traditional style such as Eagle Claw will have a basic set of principles, or key words which are the foundation for the style. The key words represent the particular features and tendencies which a style uses for de-

Figure 1

fense and attack; all of the techniques are derived from the basic principles or key words. Some styles and divisions contain a few of the same key words, but apply them a little differently. Many times poetry has been used to hand down the key words to certain students. The correct interpretation of the poetry becomes the responsibility of the student who has been given the literature. Such books of poetry containing the key words were sometimes given only to select students.

Eagle Claw as a style has itself thirteen such key words: "twist" (*jhuan*), "revolve" (*jhan*), "gesticulate" (*yeh*), "ascend" (*terng*), "clamp" (*diao*), "joining" (*kaw*), "throw" (*zen*), "movement" (*nuo*), "dodge" (*shan*), "withdraw" (*suo*), "jump" (*yaw*), "stumble" (*dye*), and "grasp" (*jaw*). Again, the meaning of these key words are usually expressed or explained in poetry. For example, one line of poetry states, "Grab the joint: twist." Eagle Claw stylists realize through these lines that everytime they grab a joint, such as the wrist, they must twist to cause the opponent pain.

Returning to Eagle Claw's history, there are no available records on the style until the Ming dynasty (1368–1644 A.D.). But during the Ming, a Shao Lin monk named Li-Chuan, who originally learned the Fan Tzu style, mixed his style with Eagle Claw to form a new system which today is known as Fan Tzu Ien Jao. Later this style passed to Tao Gi, a Shao Lin priest, who passed it to Far Cheng.

Far Cheng passed down Fan Tzu Ien Jao to Lieu Shih-Jwing. Lieu Shih-Jwing lived at the end of the Ching dynasty (1900 A.D.) as a famous Eagle Claw master in Peking. He was also very well known for his expertise in the staff. Later, one of the students that Lieu Shih-Jwing handed the style to was his nephew, Chen Tzu-Cheng. Chen became a very famous Eagle Claw master in this century. Early in this century he was invited to teach at the Shanghai Chin Woo Association. In 1924 he went to the Hong Kong Chin Woo Association where he taught until 1929. A student of his, Lieu Men-Far, went with Cheng to Hong Kong. Lieu Men-Far remained in Hong Kong after his master left and became a famous Eagle Claw instructor until his death in 1964.

The second style which is important for the Chin Na in this volume is Long Fist. As a style, Long Fist was born in this century at the Nan King Central Kuo Su Institute. The institute was set up by the Nationalist government in 1928 for the purpose of reorganizing and revitalizing Wu Su after the internal strife that resulted from the overthrow of the Chin dynasty. The Institute invited many famous Northern division masters to teach and exchange ideas. The style which was created in the Nan King Central Kuo Su Institute out of the best techniques of Northern systems has come to be known as Long Fist. One of the main styles to influence the course of study at the institute was Eagle Claw, especially its Chin Na.

The author's Long Fist master, Li Mao-Ching, studied Long Fist under Han Chin-Tan, who was himself a second generation martial artist of the Nan King Central Kuo Su Institute. In the course of learning the Long Fist style, Han Chin-Tan was also taught Eagle Claw Chin Na. Han Chin-Tan

Figure 2

had to leave the Central Kuo Su Institute in 1936 when it was closed because of the Japanese invasion of China. After leaving the Kuo Su Institute, Han Chin-Tan continued to research and improve on his knowledge
of Chin Na, thus increasing his expertise. After World War II, Han Chin-
Tan went to Taiwan where he was a famous instructor of Chin Na at the
Central Police Academy for over twenty years until his death in 1976.

Finally, the last important history which needs to be known is that of
White Crane. There exists two main divisions in White Crane: Pai Huo
Chuan and Tzon Huo Chuan. These styles are popular in Taiwan, Hong

Kong, and in the Canton area generally. Pai Huo Chuan was said to be created in Tibet by a Shao Lin monk named A Da Taou around 1796. It is said that A Da Taou developed Pai Huo Chuan while watching a snake fight a white crane. He carefully studied the strengths of each animal and from each developed effective fighting techniques and principles.

The second division of White Crane, Tzon Huo Chuan, was created by Fan Fai-Shih in the last century. After a heavy rainstorm Fan Fai-Shih watched as a white crane shook water off its body by quick, powerful jerking motions. He realized that such jerking could produce an enormous amount of power when used by humans in the correct fashion. Then Fan Fai-Shih came to develop the style. In fact, Tzon Huo can mean either shaking or jumping White Crane. Tzon Huo has fourteen key words: "pluck" (*chai*), "fly" (*fei*), "beak" (*zou*), "cover" (*gai*), "disperse" (*por*), "follow" (*shuenn*), "sticking" (*nien*), "grasp" (*kou*), "rend" (*chei*), "shaking" (*jan*), "dodge" (*shan*), "strike" (*dar*), "escape" (*dun*), and "twist" (*neu*).

In 1932 Tzon Huo Chuan was brought to Taiwan by Lin Kuo-Chong and Gin Shao-Fon. Gin Shao-Fon learned Tzon Huo from an instructor who was a student of Fan Fai-Shih (the founder): his name was Chen Shyue-Shen. The author's White Crane master, Cheng Gin-Gsao, learned Tzon Huo from Gin Shao-Fon. From Gin Shao-Fon Master Cheng learned the White Crane system of Chin Na, which emphasized cavity press and grasping the muscle; later, Cheng Gin-Gsao organized White Crane Chin Na into a systematic discipline that included herbal treatments, power and speed training, human anatomy, and new Chin Na techniques.

Finally, the author, who has learned the Eagle Claw and White Crane methods of Chin Na, has been involved in the active teaching of Chin Na since 1964. During and after that time, besides learning the two systems, the author has researched further into the area, gaining new knowledge. During these years of research the author has mixed and organized both complementary systems, taking in and adding from the best of each style new techniques and training methods. The author is currently researching and refining the mixed system.

Yeuh Fei

The Sung dynasty in China was a sorrowful time for the Chinese; wars with northern barbarians (Gin race), corruption, and hunger constantly oppressed the people. But in the midst of all these troubles there arose a man who showed by the purity of his spirit and ideals that goodness, righteousness, and loyality were qualities that still lived. For countless generations after his betrayal and murder at the hands of traitors, Marshal Yeuh Fei (fig. 2) has been a symbol for the Chinese people of the complete virtuous man; in peace Yeuh Fei was a great scholar of Chinese classics; in war Yeuh Fei was a brave and shrewd general against the enemies of his country.

Yeuh Fei was born on February 15th, 1103 A.D. in Tan Yin Hsien, Huo Nan province. During his birth a momentous event took place; while the child was being born a great powerful bird called the perng flew onto the roof and began to make tremendous noises. The father sensed that the bird's presence was an omen which foretold a tumultuous yet inspired fate for his son; the father thus named his son *Fei* which in Chinese means "to fly." This reflected the father's idea that his son would fly to great and noble heights as a man.

When Yeuh Fei was but one month old tragedy struck: the Yellow River flooded and killed his father. Yeuh Fei's mother had to save them by taking refuge in a giant urn; the urn acted as a small boat and took both mother and son to safety. When they reached dry land and the flood had receded, the mother went back to find that their home and property were totally destroyed. The mother and son were completely alone.

Although very poor, Yeuh Fei's mother, who was a well–educated scholar, possessed the courage, intelligence, and bravery to raise her son properly while giving him noble ideals. Because Yeuh Fei was too poor to pay for an education, his mother taught him personally. Each day his mother taught him how to read and write by drawing figures on the sand. Even though other children had books, pens, and paper, Yeuh Fei became one of the most educated youngsters in his village; few children could match his scholarship.

In many ways the most important person and greatest influence on Yeuh Fei's life was his mother. All the ideals that Yeuh Fei lived and died for were taught to him by his mother as they held their own classes using the sand as a blackboard. Without his mother's teachings and examples, Yeuh Fei would never have become the brave, intelligent, and loyal leader that he was.

The young Yeuh Fei was a very avid reader; among his favorite subjects were history and military theory. The book he admired and studied the most was *Suen's Book of Tactics* (*Suen Tzu Bin Far*), a book written by Suen Bin (220 B.C.) describing the theory and practice of warfare. From this book Yeuh Fei learned important principles which later helped him in his military career.

When Yeuh Fei was a young man he became a tenant farmer for a landlord named Han Chi. After long hours of work he would come home to continue studying with his mother. Yeuh Fei was much admired for this, and for the great physical strength he was showing as a young man. As in scholarship, no one could match his natural power and speed.

These admirable qualities were noticed by a certain man in the town called Chou Ton. Chou Ton himself was a scholar and a very good martial artist who had studied in the Shao Lin Temple. Seeing that Yeuh Fei possessed many noble qualities, Chou Ton began to teach him martial arts. Martial arts as it was taught to Yeuh Fei was a complete system involving barehand combat, weapons, military tactics, horsemanship, archery, and other related areas. By constant practice Yeuh Fei mastered everything Chou Ton taught.

When Yeuh Fei was nineteen years old (1122 A.D.) he decided to aid his country by joining the Chinese army in its war against the Gin, a nomadic people which had invaded the Northern Sung. The Sung dynasty, which was originally located in northern China, had to move to the south to re-establish itself with a new capital and emperor because the Gin had sacked their old capital and captured their previous emperor. The Sung which was invaded is known as the Northern Sung (960–1127 A.D.), while the Sung that established itself in the South after the Gin invasion is known as the Southern Sung (1127–1279 A.D.). For years the weakened Southern Sung had to pay bribes to the Gin to keep them from attacking further south. When Yeuh Fei joined the army, the Southern Sung was trying to regain its lost land by war.

Yeuh Fei proved himself to be a spectacular soldier. His wisdom, bravery, and martial skills earned him promotion after promotion until he became a general after six years. Later, Yeuh Fei became the head commander or marshal of the army that was assigned to fight the Gin. Once Yeuh Fei became the marshal, he instituted for his soldiers a systematic training program in martial arts. Although some martial training had previously existed, Yeuh Fei was the first to introduce Wu Su into the army as a basic requirement before combat. Many times a young man joined the army only to find himself in battle the very next day. After a while, Yeuh's troops, known as Yeuh Jar Chun became a highly efficient and successful fighting unit.

The success of Yeuh's troops can be basically attributed to three things. First, he made all his training strict; the troops were trained in a serious and professional manner. The soldiers were pushed until they excelled in martial arts. Second, Yeuh Fei set up a military organization that was efficient and well run. Third, and most important, Yeuh Fei created for his troops two new styles of Wu Su. The first style which he taught to the troops was from internal Wu Su and led to the creation of Hsing I. The second style, which he created out of external Wu Su, was Eagle Claw, a style which put a major emphasis on Chin Na. The external style, because it was learned more easily, and because it had immediately practical techniques, made Yeuh's troops successful in battle.

With his highly trained troops Yeuh Fei was in favor of pressing the attack against the Gin; Yeuh Fei was so loyal and patriotic that he felt it was shameful for the Sung to pay the Gin bribes. Yeuh Fei constantly felt intense personal agony at the humiliation that his country suffered. With the desire to free his country constantly on his mind, Yeuh Fei on his own initiative advanced his troops against the Gin to win back honor for the Sung.

When Yeuh Fei went into battle, his highly trained troops had many victories in their early march north. But in the early part of the campaign, Yeuh Fei had not yet encountered the Gin commander Wuh Jwu, who himself had never lost a battle. Wuh Jwu's terrifying success in war was on account of his main weapon—the feared Kua Tzu Ma. The Kua Tzu Ma was an ancient version of the tank; it was a three horse drawn chariot which had all the horses connected by chain and completely covered with armour; the men in the chariot were also protected by armour. The horses and soldiers thus could not be shot by arrows. As a result, the chariots were free to keep moving and its drivers free to kill.

Yeuh Fei had given much thought to defending against the awful Kua Tzu Ma. As in other cases, Yeuh's brilliant military mind came up with a solution. He found that the horses were not protected in one place—their legs; putting armour on the horses' legs would have made them immobile. It was too difficult to attack the horses' legs by conventional arrows and spears, so Yeuh Fei divised a new set of weapons. Yeuh Fei had two simple but effective weapons made: a sword with a hooked end, which was extremely sharp on the inside part of the hook, and a shield made out of a vine called "ratton" (*Tern*). This army was called the *Tern Pai Chun*, or "Ratton Shield Army."

At last, both generals met on a fateful day. When the battle started, Yeuh Fei had the Ratton Shield Army crouching very low in the path of the Kua Tzu Ma. Before the chariots could reach the soldiers, Yeuh Fei set up obstacles such as ditches and upright spears in order to slow down the Kua Tzu Ma. By slowing down the chariots, Yeuh Fei's soldiers, who were mainly on foot, could move against the enemy with more ease. As the chariots advanced the crouching men hooked and cut out the legs of the horses, thus making them fall; it was impossible for the horses to trample the crouching men because the shields were greased, the horses slipped everytime they put their legs on the shields. When the crouching soldiers attacked the horses they only had to cripple one animal to stop the chariot. Once the chariot was stopped, other soldiers surrounded it and killed the drivers. On that day Yeuh Fei scored a military victory which will live on in history and legend.

Yeuh Fei then proceeded north, regaining lost territory and defeating such Gin generals as the Tiger King and Great Dragon. But while Yeuh Fei was gaining his country's honor back, the Gin leaders themselves successfully bribed one of the most infamous men in Chinese history—Chin Kua—to stop Yeuh Fei. Chin Kua was at that time the prime minister and the most influential man at the emperor's corrupt court.

While Yeuh Fei's army moved north, Chin Kua, to achieve his evil act, decided to send an imperial order with the emperor's official golden seal (*Gin Pie*), asking Yeuh Fei to come back; according to tradition, a general fighting on the front line had the option of refusing an order of retreat. Chin Kua was counting on Yeuh Fei's patriotic sense of loyalty for the emperor to get him back. To ensure Yeuh Fei's return, Chin Kua sent twelve gold sealed orders in one day; so much pressure made Yeuh Fei return.

When Yeuh Fei returned he was immediately imprisoned. Because Chin Kua feared that any sort of trial would reveal Yeuh Fei's innocence, he ordered Ho Juh to thoroughly investigate Yeuh Fei's life in an attempt to find some excuse for the imprisonment. Ho Juh searched and searched, but he found nothing; although a powerful general, Yeuh Fei never abused his position for bad purposes. Ho Juh found that Yeuh Fei had lived a Spartan life and had fewer possessions than a peasant. When Ho Juh returned to Chin Kua, he reported only one fact of significance. When Yeuh Fei joined the army his mother tatooed on his back a certain phrase: "Be loyal and pure to serve your country" (*Ginn Chung Pau Kuo*).

With such an honest general as Yeuh Fei, Chin Kua had only one alternative; Chin Kua had Yeuh Fei's food poisoned. The noble general was viciously betrayed by his own countryman. Without the glory and honor that was his right, Yeuh Fei died in jail as a prisoner on December 27, 1141 A.D. Yeuh Fei was thirty-eight years old. Later, Yeuh Fei's adopted son, Yeuh Yun and Yeuh Fei's top assistant, Chang Shien, were also killed.

For twenty years Yeuh Fei was officially considered a criminal. But in 1166 A.D. a new and better government and emperor took control. They refused to let the treachery of Chin Kua overrule the true story of Yeuh Fei. The new emperor cleared Yeuh Fei and gave him a new burial vault and name. Yeuh Fei's new name symbolized what he always was and always will be: *Yeuh Wu Mu*—"Yeuh, the righteous and respectable warrior."

CHAPTER 2

CHIN NA
THEORY

Although Chin Na techniques vary widely in their form, use, and number, they can be separated into four basic theoretical categories: misplacing the bone, dividing the muscle, sealing the breath or vein, and cavity press. Some Chin Na techniques may use only one principle, or type, while others may use a combination of types. The first two types are fundamental and do not have overly complicated principles behind them; also, they only require external power. But the advanced Chin Na, sealing the breath or vein and cavity press, require more elaborate theory and training; the detailed explanation of the theory behind these two advanced categories will be discussed in Chapter 5.

With the theoretical background presented in this chapter, the student can understand more clearly the Chin Na that he uses. With increased understanding comes a more properly applied technique.

Misplacing the Bone

Misplacing the bone, the first type of Chin Na, involves placing great stress on the joints so as to unhinge them; unhinging the joint may range from a slight unnatural twist to total dislocation. By unhinging a joint the martial artist creates two situations which can give him control over an opponent. First, the martial artist stops movement; attacking the joint is effective because the starting point of human motion begins at the joint. If a joint is locked or misplaced it is impossible to move—the particular function of a joint will have been destroyed. Second, the martial artist creates pain. When a martial artist controls a joint he sets up a chain reaction in the surrounding muscles, nerves, and ligaments which in the end causes pain. When a Chin Na of this type is applied, the ligaments and the muscles connected to the joint will invariably be stretched, thus producing pain.

When the martial artist has applied a misplacing the bone Chin Na he will have two options: he can control a person by the pain from the joint, or he can control the person by totally stopping the functioning of the joint. The last option usually requires that the martial artist break or dislocate the joint.

Although misplacing the bone Chin Na attacks the joints, there are some joints which cannot be used. In the human body there are two types of joints: movable and immovable. Only the movable joints can be attacked in this type of Chin Na. The movable joints usually used are the finger, wrist, elbow, hip, jaw, waist, knee, and the ankle.

Dividing the Muscle

Dividing the muscle, the second type, is separated into three types: twisting, grasping, and pressing. The last two are sometimes classified by themselves under the separate heading of "grasping the muscle" (*Jua Jin*). But in this book all three will be classified under dividing the muscle. The student should thoroughly understand each type.

The twisting techniques of dividing the muscle Chin Na overextend and twist certain groups of muscles. When a muscle is overextended and twisted, it will temporarily lose its ability to function. As this happens, the movement which the muscle is responsible for will be hampered or stopped. In addition, as the muscle is extended and twisted, the nerves will be put under pressure, thus creating pain. As with misplacing the bone, this type of Chin Na will stop a particular motion and cause pain.

The grasping and pressing techniques of dividing the muscle Chin Na operate from a similar basis. First, it is necessary to understand that every muscle serves either to extend or retract a limb. This is accomplished by the muscle contracting; whether the limb extends or retracts depends on the location of the muscle. A good example of this is the biceps and triceps; one muscle is responsible for pulling the arm in, and the other for pushing it out. When any of these muscles are grasped or pulled in certain sensitive zones, they are forced into an unnatural position (the twisting techniques also force the muscles into an unnatural position). The unnatural positioning agitates the nerves, thus producing pain and local paralysis. However, there are some muscles that require pressing to produce pain and paralysis. In these cases, the nerves under the muscle receive the pressure from the martial artist's hand.

The pressing and grasping techniques do not have to be extremely accurate or precise because the aim is to attack a generally sensitive area. For this reason, the grasping and pressing categories of dividing the muscle Chin Na are sometimes considered a low form of cavity press Chin Na. Like cavity press Chin Na, these two types attack certain nerves and cavities, but unlike cavity press, these two types don't require the extensive knowledge and training that is necessary for cavity press Chin Na.

To make the grasping and pressing techniques of dividing the muscle Chin Na effective, the martial artist only requires adequate muscle or external power. The power that is needed lies mainly in the fingers, wrist, and arm. Chapter 3 will describe in detail the power and speed training methods that build up muscles for effective Chin Na.

In the grasping and pressing techniques of dividing the muscle Chin Na, there are seven zones that are used for attack. These zones are not cavities, but instead are sensitive zones that are related to the nerves passing through the general vicinity. Therefore, the zones are easily paralyzed or made to feel pain. These zones are the hand, arm, shoulder, neck, chest, waist, and leg. In this chapter only the general areas will be shown. For a description of the actual methods of grasping and pressing see Chapter 5.

On the hand itself there are several areas that can be attacked. First, along both sides of every finger the main nerves for that specific finger run their course (fig. 1, A). If any of those nerves are squeezed with sufficient power, especially near the fingertips, the whole hand may become numb; with enough power the person being attacked may faint. Second, on the back of the hand, in between the tendons that lead to the fingers (fig. 1, B), are nerves that control various parts of the hand. If the martial artist presses one of his knuckles or thumb into a nerve on the back of the hand, partial paralysis of the opponent's hand may result. Last, the middle area (fig. 1, C), between the thumb and forefinger can be pressed. This area is known as the "tiger's mouth" (Fu kou), because the nerve which passes through it originates from the large intestine and passes through the heart and lung—two vital areas. Any large concentrated power applied to this specific zone can cause unconsciousness or even death because the heart and lung will be adversely affected when the power passes through the nerves.

On the arm there are four locations that can be effectively attacked. First, on the upper forearm, near the side of the elbow joint (fig. 2, A), a group of muscles can be pressed to control the forearm and hand. Second, as in figure 3, A, the middle of the elbow joint on the front side can be pressed to produce pain and paralysis. The third area that can be pressed is slightly above the back of the elbow joint—the nerve in this region is connected with the funny bone (fig. 3, B). The fourth area as seen in figure 2, B is located on the upper part of the triceps; this area is usually pinched.

The shoulder only contains two areas that are commonly used for attack. The shoulder well (fig. 4, A), is located on the meaty part of the trapezoid muscle near the neck. The shoulder well may also be pinched to achieve the same result. The second area is located on the front side of the shoulder joint as in figure 3, C. If these areas are grasped with sufficient force, the person may either become partially paralyzed or unconscious.

On the neck there are two particularly vulnerable areas for grasping the muscle Chin Na. Slightly off to the back of the throat are sensitive neck muscles (fig. 5). These muscles are usually violently pinched. If the power of the pinch is great, the person may lose consciousness due to the severe pain. Also, the muscles on the back of the neck may be pressed (fig. 4, B). Pressing the back of the neck with enough force may cause unconsciousness.

The chest area contains two areas of attack as seen in figures 6, A and 7: the muscles in front of, and in back of the armpit. With these areas, the most effective means is to pinch or to hold for an extended time. These techniques, if applied with enough power, are very much like sealing the breath Chin Na. Both varieties attack muscles around the lungs in order to

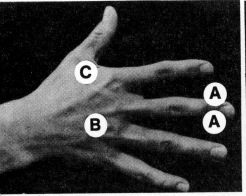

Figure 1

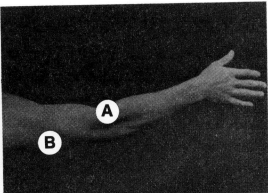

Figure 2

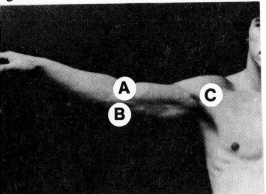

Figure 3

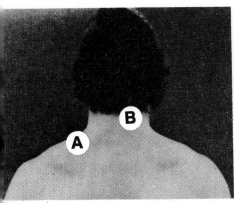

Figure 4

Figure 5

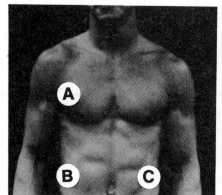

Figure 6

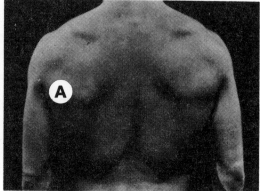

Figure 7

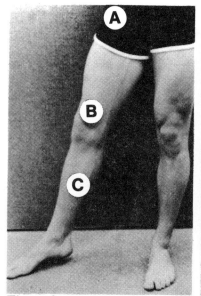

Figure 8

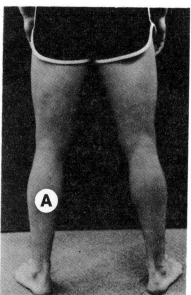

Figure 9

cause such violent contractions and pain that the person cannot adequately breathe—thus producing unconsciousness.

On the waist there are only two spots (fig. 6, B & C), and those spots can be deadly; the two areas are located on the sides below the rib cage. In ancient times it was said that certain martial artists could grab the muscles on the side of the waist and force a person to either laugh or cry. The violent fit of laughing or crying could supposedly kill because of its extremely painful nature.

The leg contains four areas for grasping the muscle. An area which is difficult to grasp is point A of figure 8, which is in front of the hip joint; to cause pain and paralysis in this area requires a good amount of power. The second area is above the knee joint (fig. 8, B), and the third is off-center of the shin (fig. 8, C). The fourth area lies in the middle of the calf as seen in figure 9.

Sealing the Breath or Vein

Sealing the breath or vein entails two separate methods: sealing the breath and sealing the vein. In sealing the breath a person is made unconscious either by breaking the wind pipe or by constricting the lungs with painful muscular contractions. Breaking the wind pipe involves only a punch or grab to the throat, while constricting the lungs is more complex. To constrict the lungs, the martial artist must have knowledge of the nerve system running through the big muscles which surround the lung. By using internal power or external penetrating power to strike the nerves, the muscle will contract with such force that the person will be rendered unconscious by the pain and the resulting inability to draw in oxygen. The general locations of the muscles involved in using this Chin Na are to be found at the solar plexus, on the shoulder blade, at the side of the chest, and at the side of the waist (see Chapter 5, "Advanced Chin Na," for detailed locations).

In sealing the vein Chin Na, a martial artist attacks the jugular vein and carotid artery on both sides of the neck in order to squeeze them shut. This in turn stops any blood from reaching the brain; within a few seconds the person will become unconscious. In this type of Chin Na (including sealing the breath), if the person is not revived he may die because the veins and arteries might remain closed for an extended time. For this reason martial artists who learn sealing the breath or vein Chin Na must also learn how to revive their unconscious victims. Additionally, the person learning this Chin Na must know Chi cycles because sealing the breath or vein is somewhat related to the time of the day, month, season, and year.

Cavity Press

The last type, cavity press, is based on directly attacking a cavity (refer to Chapter 4 for definition of a cavity) by punching, grasping, slapping, etc., in order to cause local paralysis, or if the situation arises, death. Sometimes cavity press is also referred to as "striking the blood" (*Dar Shiee*) because in attacking some cavities the major harm will result from a ruptured blood vessel. There are 108 cavities popularly used in this type of Chin Na: 72 are used for creating local paralysis or unconsciousness, while 36 are used to kill. The cavities which cause local paralysis are located on meridians (the path which the nerves take in acupuncture) which control non-vital areas such as the muscles of the arm. The death cavities, on the other hand, lie on meridians connected to internal organs, or meridians absolutely vital for the circulation of Chi, or are located in front of vital organs so that an attack will pass through the cavity and into the organs. Cavity press, like sealing the breath or vein, involves a whole complex of theory and fact which must be mastered: these will be explained in more detail in Chapter 5.

The Construction of Chin Na Techniques

Every Chin Na technique of misplacing the bone and dividing the muscle is based on certain important principles. Without these guidelines, the Chin Na techniques become fairly useless and dangerous for the martial artist who is applying them. As with every science, the basic procedures and theory have been built up by practical experience and research.

The first principle which practical applications must follow is the neutralization of the opponent's power. Before any move can be undertaken, the opponent's potential for attack must be limited or controlled; if this does not happen, then the opponent may easily pull, push, twist, or strike without an adequate defense from the martial artist. Controlling an opponent's power may sometimes only require that the martial artist turn his own palm up.

After the opponent's power has been neutralized, the martial artist must then begin his technique from a stable base. Only by having stability can a martial artist effect a fast and powerful technique. To insure that the technique is done precisely and accurately, the martial artist must have balance; without proper balance, a counterattack by the opponent is possible.

Once the technique actually begins, the movements must be simple and direct while utilizing only about one half of the martial artist's power. Overly complicated techniques that require huge amounts of power are rarely, if ever, successful. An experienced fighter from any style can readily counter inefficient and overcomplicated Chin Na techniques. If the technique requires more than half a martial artist's power, then the technique is poor. A strong opponent can overcome Chin Na techniques that require excessive power.

During the application of the Chin Na techniques, and during their finish or completion, the martial artist must make certain that all his vital zones and cavities are protected from counterattack. Many times protecting one's own vital areas involves simply standing a safe distance from the opponent. In controlling an opponent the martial artist does not want to set himself up for an easy attack.

By following and keeping in mind all of these guidelines the experienced martial artist can construct his own Chin Na techniques. But only those martial artists who are competent in theory and practice should try to make up their own techniques. Innovation has always been a vital part of Wu Su, but it can only come about through a mastery of basic skills and knowledge.

CHAPTER 3

FUNDAMENTAL TRAINING

Before the martial artist can start to effectively apply Chin Na in actual sparring situations, he must have mastered certain fundamentals of martial art. This chapter, then, will introduce aspects of Wu Su which are important for effective Chin Na. Among the things covered in this chapter will be stances, hand forms, methods for the training of power and speed, and methods for escaping from an opponent's hold. All these aspects should be mastered before attempting to use Chin Na in practical situations.

Fundamental Stances

The first prerequisite for any Chin Na technique is stability. A martial artist must have a solid foundation as a base for speedy and powerful techniques. For this reason the student must become familiar with a few stances. Once the stances are learned and mastered, the martial artist will have three advantages in his application of Chin Na: first, each Chin Na technique can be done more effectively because the weight distribution aids the person performing the technique; second, proper stances protect vital areas—the opponent cannot easily counterattack and hit sensitive areas; third, good stances improve the overall smoothness of the technique. The student should practice the stances everyday to make them natural and accurate.

1. *Ma Bu,* (fig. 1), or the "horse stance," is one of the most stable stances in Wu Su. The horse stance in this book is taken from White Crane. To form this stance begin with feet slightly beyond shoulder width. Collapse the knees down and inward until the calf and thigh form a 90 degree angle; keep the back straight. Ma Bu is commonly used to build up the power of the knees. Each day the beginning martial artist should stand in Ma Bu for at least five to ten minutes; standing in Ma Bu any longer than ten minutes will strain and injure the tendons in the knee. To practice this form, stand with feet together and hands at waist. From this position make a small jump into Ma Bu; return to original position with a hop, and then start over. Anytime Ma Bu is assumed the power from the legs should go straight down. If the power goes off to the sides, then the person is unstable.

Figure 1

2. *Deng San Bu,* (fig. 2), which means "mountain climbing," is very effective in the use of Chin Na since it brings the weight of the body forward. In
this stance 60 percent of the body's weight is put on the lead leg while 40
percent of the weight is put on the back leg. The hips are turned in the
direction of the front leg and the front foot is at a 15 degree inward angle.
To practice this stance, assume it with the right leg forward. With a swinging motion turn the hips 180 degrees counterclockwise until the left leg
becomes the lead; the left leg at this moment has 60 percent of the weight.
Turn the hips back 180 degrees clockwise so that the original position is
reassumed. Keep repeating. Each time the turn is made the weight balance
must shift.

Figure 2

3. *Dsao Pan Bu,* (figs. 3 & 4), which means "sitting on crossed legs," is very important in some Chin Na techniques because it allows the body to turn and twist. To assume this stance first stand in Ma Bu. Lift up the left toe and begin to turn counterclockwise while spinning on the left heel (fig. 3). Keep turning until the body is facing the opposite direction; the left foot is on its toes and the left knee is two inches above the ground as in figure 4. The feet must not be lifted completely off the ground at any moment. Turning to the right involves the same procedure, except the roles of the feet are reversed.

Figure 3

Figure 4

4. *Ssu Lieu Bu,* (fig. 5), which means "four-six stance," is extremely important for the effective completion of many techniques. It is commonly used to help bring an opponent down once he is controlled. This stance in its form is exactly opposite Deng San Bu. In Ssu Lieu Bu, 60 percent of the body's weight is on the back leg, while 40 percent is on the front leg. The back leg is turned inward and the front knee is bent. The lead foot is turned in at a 15 degree angle. To practice this stance, first assume it with the right leg forward. Turn 180 degrees counterclockwise and readjust the weight balance so that the right leg has 60 percent of the weight. Turn back 180 degrees clockwise into the original stance. Keep repeating.

Figure 5

Hand Forms for Chin Na

The proper form of the hand during the application of a Chin Na technique is of extreme importance. Every hand form has been constructed so that its structure allows for easy power and maneuverability. Using an improper hand form can make a Chin Na technique ineffective; this is especially true for the advanced Chin Na techniques.

For fundamental Chin Na, dividing the muscle and misplacing the bone, there are six basic hand forms that have proven to be useful. These hand forms are shown in figures 6-11. Although these are not the only hand forms that are used, they are among the most practical and popular. Some divisions will use and specialize in different hands than the ones listed.

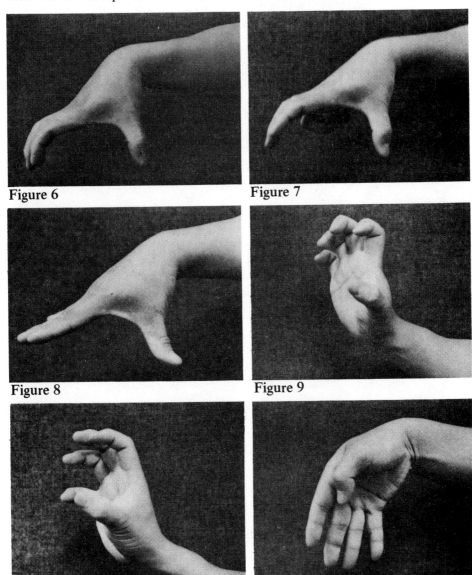

Figure 6

Figure 7

Figure 8

Figure 9

Figure 10

Figure 11

Cavity press Chin Na, unlike the fundamental types, can use practically any hand form so long as the power can concentrate and penetrate to the correct point. For this reason, even kicks can be used in cavity press. But there are hand forms that do offer greater potential for effectiveness than others. Because cavities are small points, the hand forms that are most effective for this Chin Na are those that can concentrate power to a very limited area; stiff fingers, extended knuckles, and pointed fist forms are therefore usually the best. The most useful are shown in figures 12–19. The last hand form, Secret Sword Hand, is extremely versatile because it can concentrate power to a fine point, thus making almost every cavity accessible to attack. Different divisions have their own methods of training the hand forms they specialize in. The method for training the last hand form will be explained later. For the more conventional forms, regular practice will make them effective.

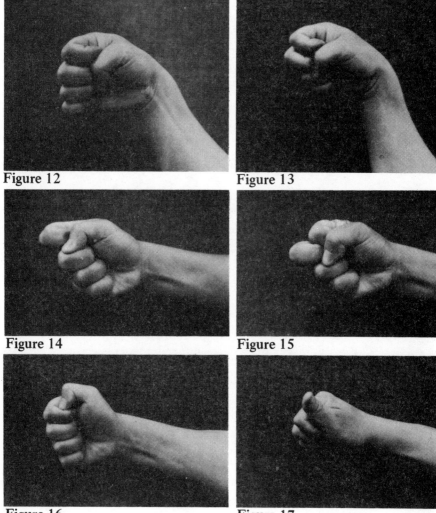

Figure 12

Figure 13

Figure 14

Figure 15

Figure 16

Figure 17

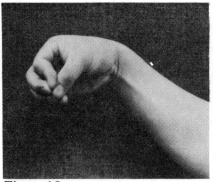
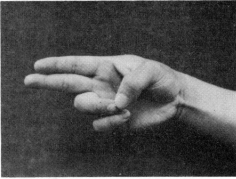

Figure 18   Figure 19

In sealing the breath or vein there are three basic hand forms that are used: Knife Hand, Palm, and Forearm. These are all variations of the open hand as shown in figure 20: Knife Hand uses point A, the Palm uses point B, and the Forearm uses points C and D. There is a special reason why sealing the breath or vein uses only three hand forms. In this Chin Na, the object is to strike a general area which is sensitive to attack. This contrasts with the hand forms used for cavity press, which are constructed to concentrate power at a specific point. By striking at a general zone with a hand form that does not specifically concentrate power at a point, the attacked region will contract or collapse as a whole, thus producing the desired effects of this Chin Na. The martial artist should keep practicing all the mentioned hand forms until he is comfortable with them.

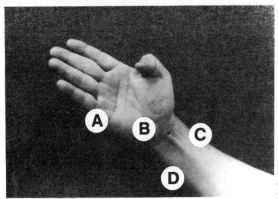

Figure 20

Power and Speed Training

While Chinese martial artists understand the primary importance of proficiency in technique, they do not underestimate the vital role of speed and power. In the Chinese martial community there is a saying that, "The fast will hit the slow and the strong will hit the weak." In some cases, a fast and powerful martial artist with poor technique may overcome an average opponent who has good technique. If a martial artist has speed but no power, his techniques will be ineffective on a slower opponent who is careful and stronger. Likewise, a martial artist who has power and little speed can be out-maneuvered by an opponent who is faster but weaker; the efficiency of one's power depends on speed. In the end, good techniques should always be fast and powerful.

Every Wu Su division has its own particular methods of building speed and power for Chin Na. Although the methods differ, the final goal is the same. In the practice of speed, power, and reaction there are methods which develop the eyes, hands, arms, shoulders and waist. Other methods develop the ability to dodge, escape, and withdraw. Usually all the methods must be done with a partner to get better results. An important aspect of most training drills is that they develop the speed and power muscles simultaneously. This is important because, physically, the body has separate muscles which are used only for speed or only for power; it is thus an advantage to have one drill which develops both types.

As the student performs each speed and power drill, one trait is developed regardless of method; that trait is mental reaction. A martial artist needs a quick mind before any block, attack, or dodging maneuver can begin. Speed and power are useless without a fast mind to guide them. Mental reaction may then be thought of as a sixth sense; by constant practice the student develops correct instinctive judgments of situations. Much of this ability comes from the experience a student gains while practicing the drills with others. There is a proverb which illustrates this idea: "A good master can teach everything to a student except experience."

Hand and Fingers

In some divisions such as Tiger, Eagle Claw, Praying Mantis, and White Crane the training of the hands and fingers for grasping is of major importance—sometimes constituting the majority of their training exercises. With constant practice of hand and finger drills the student should be able to more effectively block, hook, lock, apply Chin Na, and prevent escapes by grabbing. Concentration during these training exercises is very important.

The most popular training method for the development of hand and fingers is catching heavy falling objects in midair. Figures 21 and 22 show one application of this method: a heavy brick is dropped and then quickly caught with the hands. Start catching a brick of about twenty pounds and progressively use more weight as time goes on. When the student practices this method, first lift the brick to the stomach and let it drop. Before attempting to grasp the brick, raise both hands above the head. Once the hands are raised, move them down and grab the brick before it hits the ground. Once this form can be repeated with ease, attempt to clap the hands over the brick before grasping it; clap one, two, or three times. If the practitioner can clap his hands three times before catching the falling brick, he will have built a solid foundation for complex techniques which involve grabbing or holding. In ancient times a jar partly filled with sand was used for this exercise; as the student became more proficient the jar had sand added to it.

Figure 21   Figure 22

Another method of increasing hand power is by doing push-ups while supporting the weight of the body on the fingers. As the practitioner pushes up he should clap his hands one, two, or three times directly under his chest and then return to the original position (weight on finger tips). This method trains speed in addition to power (fig. 23-24).

Figure 23

Figure 24

A very important method of training grasping power used by Eagle Claw, White Crane, and Tiger divisions is the technique of grasping empty air. In this type of training it is particularly important that the student concentrates. An Eagle Claw method is shown in figures 25, 26, and 27. To start, stand in Ma Bu with both hands in a fist (palm up) at the waist. Move the right hand outward with the fingers pointing up and the palm facing the body (fig. 25). This move is an inside block. As the hand reaches the face level, point the fingers forward in the shape of an eagle claw (fig. 26). Slowly clench the eagle claw around your imagined enemy's wrist and pull your hand back to your waist. As the student clenches he should do it knuckle by knuckle to develop concentration power. As the right hand is returning to the waist, turn the body to the right changing the stance to Deng San Bu while punching out with the left arm (fig. 27). After the punch, switch the stance to Ma Bu and open the left fist while moving the hand counterclockwise in a half-circle. Form an eagle claw, pull, and punch out with the right arm while turning left and switching to Deng San Bu. Return to the original Ma Bu position and begin again with the extended right hand. White Crane stylists use the same method except that the White Crane Wing is used for the Eagle Claw.

Figure 25   **Figure 26**   **Figure 27**

The Tiger division has a similar type of training called *Bai Bar Chuar* which means "one-hundred grasps." Begin this form with fists at the waist while standing in Ma Bu. Strike out with both hands with palms opened. Using both hands, make two small circles in front of the body so that the hands criss-cross each other (fig. 28). The right hand moves clockwise and the left hand moves counterclockwise. When the hands are criss-crossed as in figure 28, turn them out and parallel (fig. 29). Make a Tiger Claw and slowly clench the hand knuckle by knuckle. During the clenching, the hand must be perpendicular to the forearm.

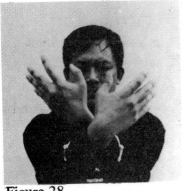

Figure 28   Figure 29

Finally, a method which can be practiced anywhere is the quick clenching and unclenching of the fist. In this method the student simply attempts to make as many fists as possible within a limited time. To effectively perform this, the fist should be completely closed and then opened wide. As a goal, the student should try to make 180 fists within 30 seconds (fig. 30, 31).

Figure 30   Figure 31

Wrists, Arms, and Shoulder

Finger and hand power is relatively useless without the strength of the wrist and arm. After a martial artist has grabbed an opponent, the ability to hold and control him requires wrist and arm power; otherwise the opponent can easily escape. The easiest method of building up wrist and arm power is to hold some type of heavy rod at its center and slowly move it up and down while keeping the hand relatively stationary at the hips (fig. 32). As the student improves, he should hold the rod closer to the end, thus increasing the weight of swinging.

A method used by White Crane to strengthen the wrist, arm, and shoulder is to stick two large bamboo poles (at least ten yards long) vertically in the ground about two feet apart. The student then tries to climb the poles while holding one in each hand. An advanced student will put soap or grease on his hands while climbing. This method also trains grasping power.

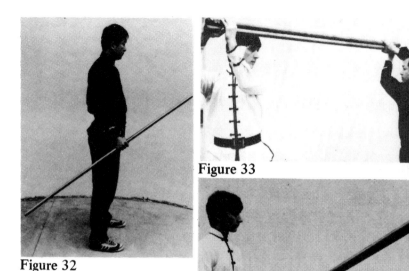

Figure 32

Figure 33

Figure 34

A popular White Crane method to build up the wrist and arms is to use two rods or several bamboo poles. In figure 33, both partners hold the rods in a tandem position as tightly as possible. Each side then swings the rods down and up in a clockwise motion. Once the rods are up to the opposite side, swing them down and up in a counterclockwise motion so that they are once again in their original position. Repeat numerous times. A variation of this is shown in figure 34. One side attempts to hold the tandem position without moving while the other side spins his body counterclockwise or clockwise; both sides must maintain their grip as tightly as possible. The side that has the rods slip from their position is the loser.

Also within White Crane is a method called "Rubbing Hands" (*Mou Sou*). This method is important for developing skill in Chin Na techniques. To begin, one student forms a White Crane Wing with his right hand and hooks the wrist of another person. The student whose wrist is hooked should have his fingers facing up and palm pointed inward as shown in figure 35. For easier reference the student dressed in the black top will be referred to as "B," while the student in the white top will be "W." From the original position, the object of W is to counteract the Wing by himself hooking the opponent with a White Crane Wing as in figure 36. As W attempts to do this he must pull or jerk back his hand using waist power; it is not possible to hook B's hand without using waist power because each time that W attempts to apply the White Crane Wing, B will attempt to stop this by also jerking with waist power. In Rubbing Hands, waist power must be used for the exercise to be effective. When W has pulled enough he must quickly turn his hand toward B's wrist. Both students will be able to feel when W has succeeded in applying the Wing. When W has succeeded in applying the White Crane Wing, B must turn his hand so that his fingers point up and palms face in (W's original position) and attempt to hook W. This training must be done vigorously and continuously.

Figure 35

Figure 36

A method that a student can practice alone is shown in figures 37 and 38. Start with the right hand around the left wrist (fig. 37). Move the left hand to the inside as in figure 38 and grab the right wrist. Repeat the same procedure with the right hand: move it to the inside and grab the left wrist. This motion results in a constant grabbing of the wrists. The student should apply as much resistance to the grabbing as possible.

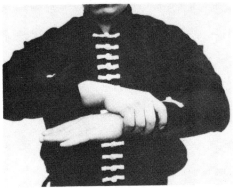
Figure 37

Figure 38

Finally, a good way to build upper arm and shoulder strength is to move in various directions by assuming a low push-up position as in figure 39. From this position the student can move forward, backward, or to the side (fig. 40). Only one direction should be practiced at a time. In moving to any direction the knees must be locked and the arms should be bent as low as possible without making the body touch the ground—the arms should never be straight. To move forward simply drag the body along in that direction using only the arms; the legs cannot help to propel the body forward. To move backward simply push away from the front, again using only the arms. To move laterally, the arms and legs on the same side must move simultaneously in the desired direction (fig. 40). If the student wishes, he may do all these forms supporting his weight on the fingers.

Figure 39

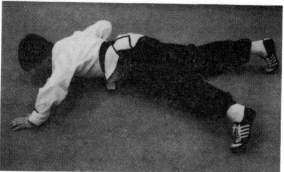
Figure 40

Neutralization of Pressure

Aside from punching and kicking, an opponent can exert pressure on a martial artist by roughly four methods: an opponent may grab, embrace, push, or press. When an opponent pressures the martial artist in any of these ways, the power or momentum of the enemy must be rendered inefficient or neutralized. If the pressure from the opponent is not neutralized, then the martial artist is vulnerable to Chin Na techniques and other kinds of attack. This section, then, will show techniques that are used to neutralize the pressure from an opponent whose purpose is to apply Chin Na or whose purpose is to first push or grab before punching or kicking.

In practicing the neutralization techniques of this chapter, two considerations are very important during training sessions. First, always practice with a partner. By using a partner, the martial artist will get firsthand experience: experience is always the best teacher. Second, the ability to dissolve and neutralize an opponent's power must be through instantaneous feeling, and not by sight. The martial 'artist must keep practicing until his reaction comes naturally without the excessive use of eyesight to determine the nature of the opponent's pressure.

The first way that an opponent can exert pressure is by grabbing the wrist, arm, or clothes: these three areas are the most commonly grabbed. When the martial artist is grabbed there are basically five ways to dissolve or neutralize the opponent's power. The five ways of neutralization are called "dissolve down," "dissolve up," "dissolve by turning," "side push," and "following the limb." Each of these methods stops the pressure from the opponent while also helping to set up the enemy for a Chin Na technique.

The first common situation that a martial artist can find himself in is when his opponent uses an equal arm grab. An equal arm grab is the right hand of an opponent grabbing the right arm of the martial artist. The grab does not necessarily have to be at the wrist or hand. It can be anywhere along the length of the arm. No matter where the grab takes place on the arm, the principles of neutralization will be the same. An opponent may grab an equal arm by two methods: first, he may grab the arm from the top as in figure 41, or second, the opponent may grab the arm from underneath as in figure 42. Both situations require separate methods of neutralization. Although only the right hand methods will be covered, the same principles and techniques would apply to a situation where a left hand grabs a left arm.

Figure 41

Figure 42

In the following descriptions of equal arm grab neutralization techniques (including the other descriptions), the martial artist dressed in the black top will be called "B," and the martial artist in the white top will be called "W."

1. Dissolve Up (fig. 43)

Starting from figure 41, B moves his arm straight up. In the process of moving the arm up, W's forearm becomes twisted so that he has little leverage to exert power.

Figure 43

2. Dissolve by Turning (fig. 44)

From figure 41, B swings his hand clockwise. W cannot hold on because B created an awkward positon for W's hand to effectively maintain power. In addition, B moved his hand into W's fingers, which are one of the weak points of a grip. The palm area is usually the strongest part of a grip—for this reason escaping from a grip involves breaking out through the thumb or fingers.

Figure 44

3. Follow the Limb (fig. 45)

Starting from figure 41, B moves his hand down and in. W's grip will slip off.

Figure 45

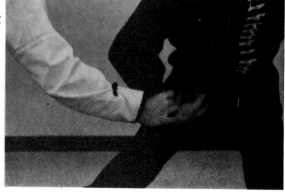

4. Side Push (fig. 46)

From figure 41, B swings his hand up, out, to the side. W cannot maintain his grip from this position.

Figure 46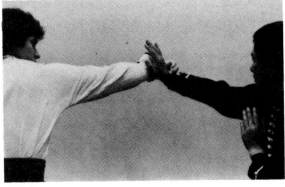

5. Dissolve Down (fig. 47)

The dissolve down technique starts the methods to neutralize an equal arm grab when the opponent grabs from underneath. From figure 42, B moves his hand straight down over W's wrist. By moving the whole hand against W's thumb, B is able to release himself.

Figure 47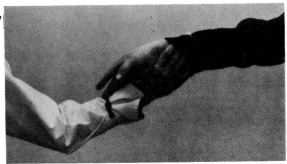

6. Following the Limb (fig. 48)

Starting from figure 42, B moves his arm straight in. By moving his whole hand away from W's fingers, B loosens W's grip.

Figure 48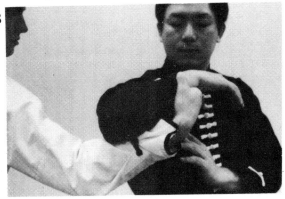

7. Side Push (fig. 49)

Starting from figure 42, B swings his hand down, up, and to the side. W will not be able to maintain his grip as B moves into his thumb.

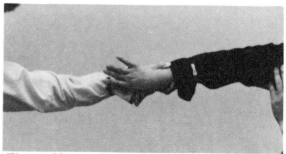

Figure 49

The second type of pressure by grabbing which can be exerted by an opponent is an opposite hand grab. This is a left hand grabbing a right arm or vice versa. As in the equal arm grab, the opponent may grab from the top (fig. 50), or from underneath (fig. 51). The following are the methods for the neutralization of the opposite grab.

Figure 50

Figure 51

1. Dissolve Up (fig. 52)

Starting from figure 50, B moves his arm up and in. B slips out of W's fingers.

Figure 52

2. Dissolve by Turning (fig. 53)

From figure 50, B swings his hand down, up, and out. B moves his whole hand into the open area of W's grip.

Figure 53

3. Dissolve Down (fig. 54)

Starting from figure 51, B pushes his hand down and over W's wrist. B's whole hand moves against W's thumb.

Figure 54

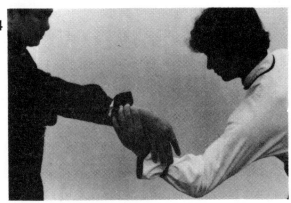

4. Following the Limb (fig. 55)

Starting from figure 51, B moves the arm down and in. W's fingers will start to slip off.

Figure 55

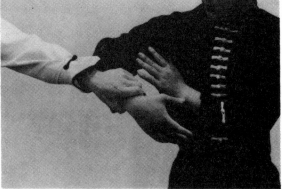

The third grabbing situation which can exist is when an opponent uses both of his hands to grab one arm as in figure 56. This combination of an equal arm grab and of an opposite hand grab will be referred to as a double hand grab. The neutralization of the double hand grab usually requires a combination of different methods. The following are two methods to break the double hand grab.

1. Following the Limb and Dissolve Up (fig. 56, 57, 58)

W grabs B with both hands: W's right hand is on top (fig. 56). B moves his arm in—this loosens the grip of W's left hand as seen in figure 57. Immediately, B swings his arm up to neutralize W's right hand (fig. 58). From this positon B can either set himself free or apply a Chin Na technique.

Figure 56

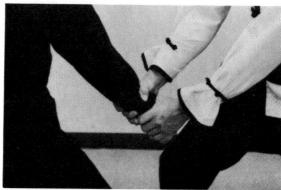

Figure 57

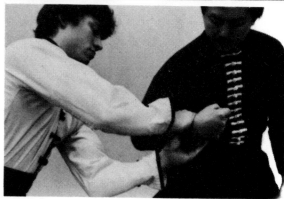

Figure 58

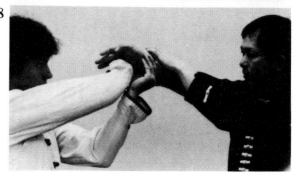

2. Dissolve Up and Side Push (fig. 59, 60, 61)

In figure 59, W has grabbed B's arm with both hands. W's left hand is on top (opposite of previous technique). B squats into a low Ssu Lieu Bu while swinging his arm up (fig. 60). B must get low to have leverage. W's left hand has nearly lost the grip with this move. B then immediately swings his arm down and to the side as in figure 61.

Figure 59

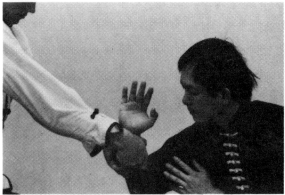

Figure 60

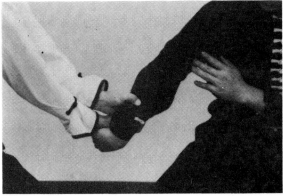

Figure 61

The second major category of pressure which an opponent may exert is the embrace. Embracing involves wrapping one or two arms around a person. The embrace is usually around the chest, abdomen, or neck, with the person most often applying the embrace from the rear. With any embrace around the chest, the martial artist must do two things immediately: first, he must inhale deeply and second, he must tighten and expand forward all the muscles of the upper body. By doing these things it is more difficult for the opponent to squeeze the person into unconsciousness. If the embrace is around the neck, two immediate actions are also required. First, one hand must come up immediately to block the embrace. Second, the martial artist must turn his neck into the triceps of the embracing arm; by doing this only the *side* of the neck is exposed to pressure, and not the weaker and vulnerable throat. The side of the neck can withstand more pressure than the throat. Following are the methods to resolve embraces to the chest and neck.

1. Groin Attack

When B is embraced around the chest, he immediately inhales, expands his muscles, and swings his hand down into W's groin (fig. 62). These are all done simultaneously. Another version is for B to kick up into W's groin (fig. 63).

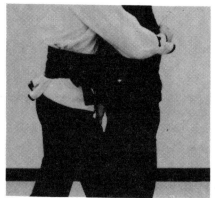

Figure 62

Figure 63

2. Leg Attack

In addition to attacking the groin, B can kick W's shin or toes as in figures 64 and 65. Again, B must inhale and expand his muscles against a chest embrace. The breathing and muscle expansion must be done simultaneously with the kick.

Figure 64   Figure 65

3. Abdomen Attack

In this situation B is grabbed around the neck. B's first move is to swing his hand up to prevent W from completing his embrace (fig. 66). Next, B turns into W's triceps and elbows him in the side (fig. 67). B can then set himself free.

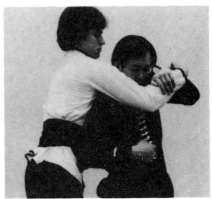

Figure 66   Figure 67

The third major category of pressure from an opponent is the push. Pushing simply involves an attempt to knock a person off balance by any type of shove. The neutralization of a push is relatively simple, although perfecting the techniques will require extensive practice because timing and coordination must be precise. The techniques against a push may also be used for a press. The following are two techniques for resolving a push.

1. Side Push

As W pushes, B turns his waist and swings up his arms until they are on the other side of B's arm; this situation is shown in figure 68. It is vital that B turns his waist in order to deflect W's power. When B feels W's power going to the side, B grabs W's hand and steps back pulling W forward (fig. 69). B's left hand is pushing down over W's elbow.

Figure 69

Figure 68

2. Dissolve Up

As W attempts to push, B raises both hands up on the inside of W's arms (fig. 70). The power of the push is resolved to the side and up.

Figure 70

CHAPTER 4

MASSAGE

Massage has long been an important part of martial training and knowledge. In the Wu Su community, massage is intimately related to the methods of healing bruises, eliminating pains such as headaches and pinched nerves, reviving unconscious persons, stimulating the function of internal organs, increasing blood circulation, and the stopping of inflammation. But in general, for martial arts the most important purpose of massage is for emergency use. Any time a student gets knocked out, dislocates a bone, pulls a muscle, or gets bruises, massage must be used. Usually herbal remedies are used in conjunction with massage. With such wide use of massage it is not surprising that its techniques are founded on some principles of Chinese medicine. In fact, enormous contributions to Chinese medicine have been made by martial artists in their investigation of sparring injuries, pressure points, herbs, exercise drills, Chi, and human anatomy. This chapter, then, will first introduce the idea of Chi and its relation to the human body. Next, the all important concept of a "cavity" (*Hsueh*), will be explained. A correct understanding and mastery of any type of Chin Na will require the complete comprehension of this concept. After defining a cavity, the chapter will go on to discuss the relationship between cavities and bruises. The last section will show the practical application of massage.

Chi

A very common concept in the Chinese martial community, but a little known and misunderstood concept in the West, is the idea of Chi. A working knowledge of Chi is very important because without it the martial artist could not understand such things as internal power, meditation, massage, and striking points.

The best way to begin an understanding of Chi is to see it in relation to the circulatory and nervous system. The circulatory system keeps the body alive by transporting essential ingredients such as food and oxygen to every single part of the body. Only one other system is as extensive as the circulatory system—the nervous system. In fact, it is usually the case that veins, arteries, and major nerves follow the same path through the body.

The blood may be thought of as the vital principle in the circulatory system because it is the active part responsible for the maintenance of life. Because the circulatory system runs through the entire body, the vital principle (blood) also runs through the entire body. If the nervous system is equally important to the body and as extensive as the veins and arteries, does the nervous system, then, also have a vital principle which circulates through the body? Three thousand years of Chinese medicine have answered "yes."

The vital principle which circulates through the pathways of the nervous system is Chi. Chi plays a role similar to blood, but differs in that it is a type of electrical energy. Chi, more than the blood, is responsible for keeping a person alive. Chi is the life force which all living things possess. Of course, Western science does not accept these concepts of Chi, but the existence of Chi is nonetheless true.

Chi, like blood, circulates in the body on a regular basis. However, Chi also circulates in cycles of days, months, seasons, and years, while blood has a fairly constant circulation independent of time and season. These cycles usually have various pathways through the body; at certain points of the paths, the circulation of Chi can be easily affected. If at any time the circulation of Chi is slowed down or stopped, the person will become sick or die depending on which cycle of Chi is affected and to what extent. Some Chi cycles are more sensitive and vital than others.

Chi is extremely important to the martial artist for various reasons. The first reason is the matter of health. If a person can achieve a smooth continuous flow of Chi through the body, then many forms of illness will never occur. The smooth circulation of Chi is usually obtained by the calm and highly concentrated mind that comes about through meditation or Tai Chi Chuan. This is why many non-martial artists in China perform Tai Chi—to obtain a smooth circulation of Chi.

The second important aspect of Chi for the martial artist is its ability to be used as a tremendous source of power. Chinese martial artists have found that when Chi is properly channeled and concentrated, the feats of power that can be performed are over and above ordinary muscle strength or external power. (The power generated by Chi is commonly called "internal power.")

Although Chi is an enormous source of strength, few people have reached levels where Chi can be effectively used. Two obstacles stand in the way of tapping the potential of Chi. First, before a martial artist can attempt anything he must have a fluent flow of Chi through the body; this demands time and extreme patience. When the martial artist has a smooth circulation of Chi through meditation or Tai Chi Chuan, he then must find a master who can teach him how to use the Chi. The methods which develop the uses of Chi are long and difficult. The martial artist must spend at least ten years in the total process. While the concept of Chi is not extremely difficult to understand, its cultivation and use demand a lifetime of work.

Theory of Massage

The key point in the understanding of massage is the concept of a cavity. Cavities are intimately related to the circulation of Chi through the nervous system. At certain points on the body the nerves, which are the pathways for the circulation of Chi, can be easily stimulated because they usually lack adequate protection by bones, muscles, ligaments, and tendons. By stimulating those spots, the circulation of Chi can be altered for good or bad results.

Cavities are the gates through which various parts of the body are stimulated or depressed. A cavity, after all, is an exposed part of a general nerve system, and the nerve is intimately connected with other parts of the body. For example, one nerve path in the arm is connected to the lungs. These specific nerve systems and their connections are called meridians in Chinese acupuncture. The cavities on the meridians are the points where Chinese doctors stick their acupuncture needles.

In Chinese acupuncture there are twelve meridians that are associated with various organs and two vessels which help in overall functioning. These meridians and vessels are the stomach, triple burner, small intestine, large intestine, heart, liver, pericardium, spleen, kidney, bladder, gall bladder, lung, conception vessel, and governing vessel. On these 14 pathways lie more than 700 cavities that are used in acupuncture to cure various sorts of illness. But of the 700 cavities, martial artists use only 108 cavities for the purposes of attack; some acupuncture cavities are not used because they are too small, require too much power to affect, or are located in areas not practical to attack. Of the 108 cavities used for martial purposes, 72 are used to create unconsciousness, local paralysis, or pain, while the remaining 36 are used for killing.

In the process of stimulating a cavity, the Chinese acupuncture specialist can gently agitate certain internal organs in order to produce better health and vigor. But if a cavity is overstimulated as in a physical attack, the effect may be dangerous because overstimulation may cause violent contractions of the organs or muscles controlled by the meridian. The final effect of stimulating a cavity, depends on such things as the connections of meridians, the amount of power used, the depth of cavity, the time of day, month, season, or year, and the type of technique used to stimulate the cavity. These principles are used by the Chinese acupuncturist and the Chinese martial artist.

Basically, there are three types of cavities. The first type of cavity occurs when two muscles touch or intersect each other in such a manner that a small depression or hole is created at the point of intersection or touching; to create the depression the muscles may either cross over, parallel, converge into, or diverge away from each other. Usually, the meridians lie under a protective layer of muscle, but at points where two muscles cross, converge, diverge, or parallel, a meridian may become exposed. An example of this can be seen in figure 1, A. The radial nerve, as it passes into the forearm, becomes exposed due to an overlapping of muscles in that area. The majority of the cavities are of this type.

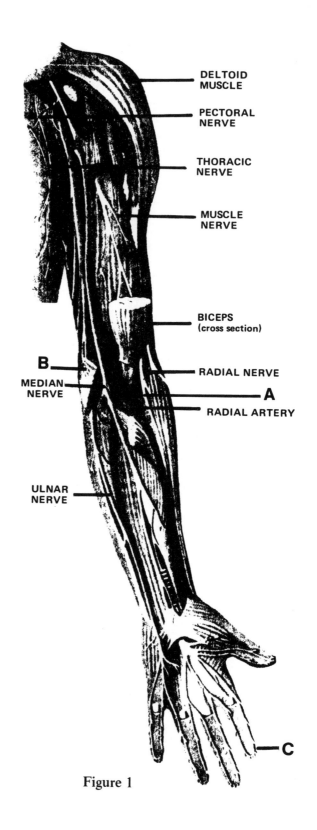

DELTOID
MUSCLE

PECTORAL
NERVE

THORACIC
NERVE

MUSCLE
NERVE

BICEPS
(cross section)

B

RADIAL NERVE

MEDIAN
NERVE

A

RADIAL ARTERY

ULNAR
NERVE

C

Figure 1

The second type of cavity occurs when a nerve is exposed in an area lacking much muscle. The nerve in these areas is naked in that there is little to protect it. An example of this type of cavity is shown in figure 1, B. In the picture the cavity is created behind the point indicated. The ulnar and radial nerves lie relatively unprotected on the elbow bone because no heavy layers of muscle are over them. Because of their exposed nature, these types of cavities can cause an extremely sharp pain if they are directly hit. An example of this (the cavity referred to in figure 1, B) is the funny bone.

The third type of cavity lies under a protective layer of muscle, but can still be effectively stimulated because of its natural sensitivity. An example of this type of cavity is shown in figure 1, C. Usually these cavities have only a thin or fair layer of muscle over them, but at the same time are very near the surface of the body. For this reason they can be stimulated with relative ease even though they are under muscle tissue. In figure 1, C it is easy to see that the nerves running along the sides of fingers have some protection, but still not enough to guard against stimulation. This type of cavity can also be felt on the side of the biceps.

What then, is the particular relationship of cavities to massage? First, any time a person physically exerts himself for a period of time (for example a Wu Su practice) he creates acid as a waste product in the muscles. Given time and rest, the body will flush out the acid, but if the acid reaches a cavity it will stay there longer than normal. The acid will eventually leave the cavity, but more slowly in comparison to the acid in the muscle. While the acid is in the cavity it will interfere with Chi circulation and cause soreness. By massaging the cavity, the acid is forced into the surrounding tissue where it is more easily flushed out.

The same principle applies for bruises. When a bruise occurs it may travel or spread into a cavity and affect Chi circulation. But bruises, unlike acid, may stay in the cavities for longer periods of time; the time may be from a few days to a few years. For this reason, masage is necessary to force the bruise out of the cavity and into the surrounding tissue, which can heal the bruise more quickly. If the bruises are not forced out, they may cause trouble. The older a person gets, the more trouble they cause. In addition, some bruises can be serious in that they can completely stop the circulation of Chi. Some bruises in vital cavities may cause death.

A basic tenet underlying the removal of acid and bruises from a cavity is the belief that massage is a way of helping the body to recover on its own. In Chinese medicine this approach is very fundamental. The idea is not to impose an outside cure, but to help the operating forces of the body in order that a natural recovery can take place. Western medicine usually operates on the opposite principle: force a cure on the patient.

An example of this difference in principle can be seen in the cure of serious bruises. On a severe bruise that is beginning to swell a Chinese herbalist will use massage and herbs to diffuse as much of the bruise as possible. By diffusing the bruise the body can better cope with the injury because it is not concentrated in one place; it is easier for the body to cure a diffused bruise than one concentrated bruise. But in the same case Western medicine will use ice to contain the swelling and bruise in one spot. This may contain the bruise and stop the symptom of swelling, but it has done nothing to cure the bruise itself. The notion is that by forcing the symptoms to go away the patient is cured.

Application of Massage

Many methods and techniques of massage exist in the martial community and around the world. In Japan a large number of techniques are done with the finger tips, while in Greece a branch is used to lightly whip the body. The whipping stimulates many surface nerve endings causing the muscles to relax; a slight agitation of the nerves has a calming effect. By relaxing the muscles, the bruises and accumulated acid can be flushed out with more ease because the relaxed muscles permit the blood to flow more efficiently in the sore areas.

For massage to be effective the student should understand some important points. Massage, besides being used for emergency purposes, is a useful teaching device for martial students. When two students are engaged in massage, each is gaining a knowledge of human anatomy. By massaging they learn where the major cavities are and the amount and depth of power needed to affect the cavities. In addition, they gain firsthand information on the location of muscles and the structure of joints. Such overall knowledge is invaluable for the martial artist.

During any massage the concentration of the masseur (the one performing the massage techniques) is important. Because cavities exist at various depths and vary in their response to pressure, the masseur must be able to focus his power correctly—this requires concentration. If a masseur is not in the right mental and emotional state, his effectiveness will be diminished. For example, if he is upset or angry he may press too hard.

In a manner related to concentration, the person who is being massaged must relax. To help himself relax, the student being massaged should be clean before the session starts; cleaning up calms the mind. If the student being massaged becomes tense during the massage, the masseur should gently move his fingers over the other's body: this will produce a light smooth sensation. In gently moving the hands over the body, the masseur should not tickle the other person because tickling causes the muscles to tense up and disrupt relaxation. If a person is naturally ticklish the masseur can begin with a massage that is very soft and gradually build up to more power. In this way the ticklish person, over a period of time, will accommodate himself to more stimulation.

Before the beginning of the massage session, each student must be willing to cooperate with his partner; this cooperation is very important. It is necessary for the students to let each other know whether certain techniques are causing pain or are ineffective. Without communication the students will not know whether they are successfully getting the right areas. If one student is massaging too hard and the other does not let him know, then the excess pressure may worsen any existing bruises on the student being massaged. In addition, people vary in their sensitivity and in their location of certain cavities and muscles: there is no set formula in what technique to use or how much pressure to apply because each individual is unique. If no communication exists, the student who is massaging cannot adjust his techniques to suit the other's individual needs.

During the massage it is important that the muscles are not massaged against the grain. The rubbing, pushing, pulling, etc., must follow the natural contours of the body. For example, the calf muscles should not be massaged sideways, but up and down; by going against the grain the muscle fibers are being pulled apart. In a related manner, the masseur should not rub the skin only. When massaging the masseur should plant his fingers in one spot and then move the underlying muscles; even though the fingers are planted on one spot of the skin, they still can move around because of the skin's elastic nature.

Finally, photographs (fig. 2–44) will help the student in giving him an indication of useful massage techniques and the areas to which they are applied. To find the locations of cavities the student should consult the list of acupuncture books given at the end of the chapter. As a final point, the student should experiment with different types of hand forms on other areas of the body for which they were indicated; it is important that massage fit the individual.

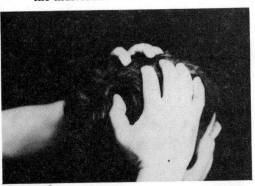

Figure 2

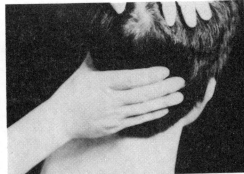

Figure 3

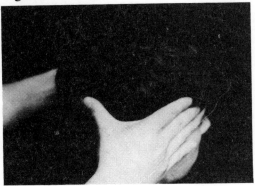

Figure 4

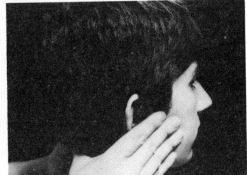

Figure 5

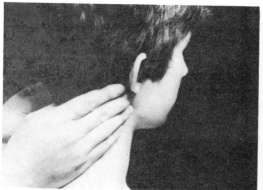

Figure 6

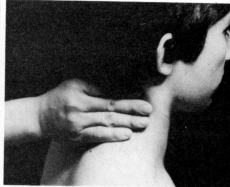

Figure 7

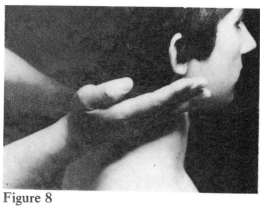

Figure 8

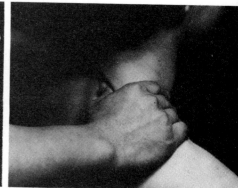

Figure 9

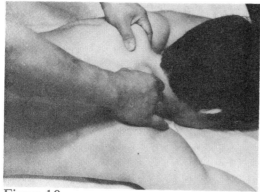

Figure 10

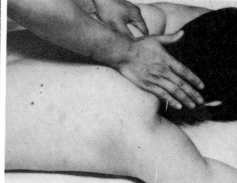

Figure 11

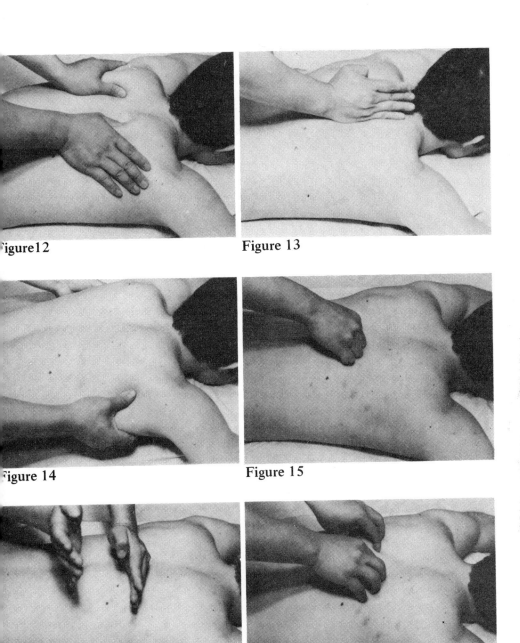

Figure 12

Figure 13

Figure 14

Figure 15

Figure 16

Figure 17

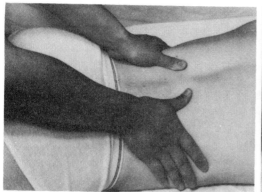

Figure 18

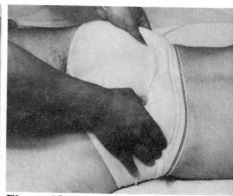

Figure 19

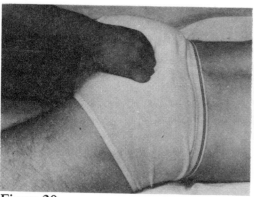

Figure 20

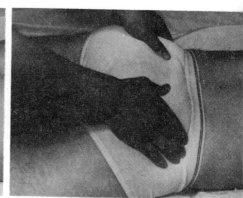

Figure 21

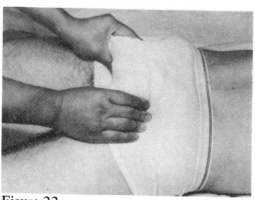

Figure 22

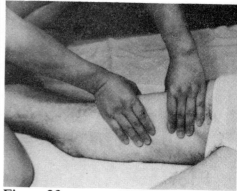

Figure 23

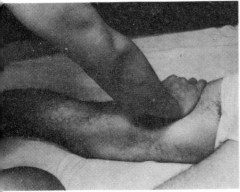

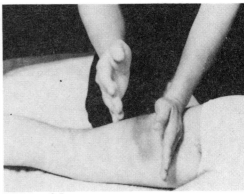

Figure 25

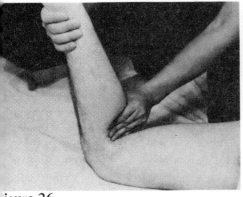

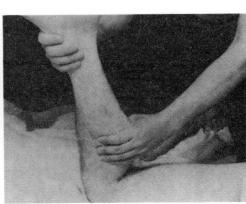

Figure 27

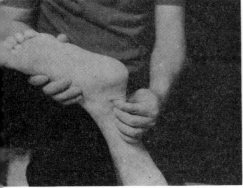

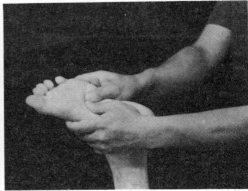

Figure 29

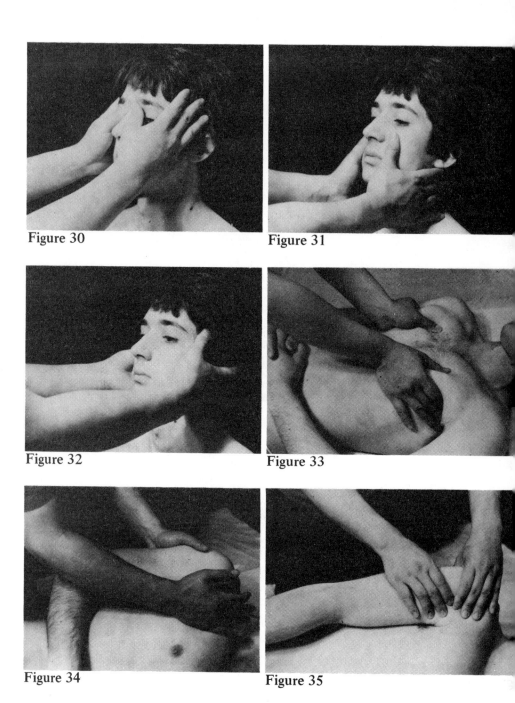

Figure 30

Figure 31

Figure 32

Figure 33

Figure 34

Figure 35

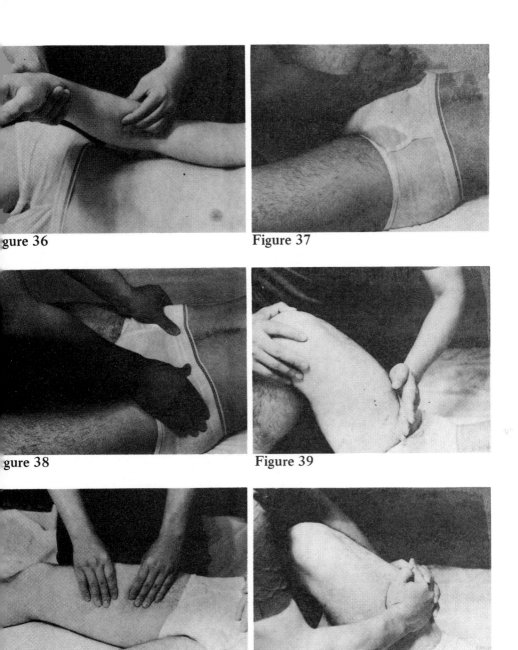

gure 36

Figure 37

gure 38

Figure 39

gure 40

Figure 41

63

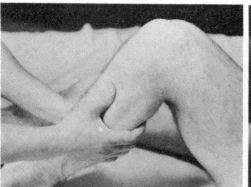

Figure 42

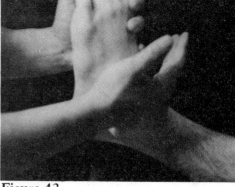

Figure 43

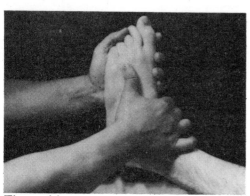

Figure 44

Bibliography

Austin, Mary. *Acupuncture Theory.* Asi Publishers, 1972.

Chu, David and Dorothy. *The Principles of Chinese Acupuncture Medicine.* Rainbow Printing, 1975.

Mann, Felix. *Acupuncture: The Ancient Chinese Art of Healing and How It Works Scientifically.* Random House, 1971.

Silverstein, Martin Elliot. *Acupuncture and Moxibustion.* Schochen Books, 1975.

Tan, Leong T. *Acupuncture Therapy: Current Chinese Practice.* Temple University Press, second edition, 1976.

CHAPTER 5

CHIN NA TECHNIQUES

In this chapter the explanations for fundamental and advanced Chin Na will be shown in detail. The first section will show the fundamental techniques of misplacing the bone and dividing the muscle, plus the areas and methods of attack for grasping the muscle. There will be explanations for seventy-one fundamental techniques of which fifteen are grasping the muscle. The section on fundamental Chin Na will contain a discussion on first aid and curative methods for injuries which can be obtained during practice. The section on first aid will show methods on the relocation of dislocated bones and a general discussion on herbs.

The second part of this chapter will explain the theory and training methods of sealing the breath or vein and cavity press. This section will show thirty-six cavity press points and ten techniques of sealing the breath or vein. This section will also contain a discussion on the methods used to revive victims of the advanced techniques.

As the martial artist reads and begins to practice the Chin Na in this book, he should realize two important points. First, the techniques in this chapter are only formulas. It is up to the martial artist to keep practicing and discussing with others the practical applications of techniques under differing circumstances. The forms must be made alive and useful.

Second, in the explanation of the fundamental techniques only one side of the technique is shown. Every technique can be equally applied to the opposite hand. Every fundamental technique has a mirror; it is only necessary for the attacker and the defender to switch hands. But in the advanced techniques of Chin Na, this situation is not always true; some advanced techniques cannot be switched to the opposite side to obtain the same results. Some cavity press techniques are specially designed to attack certain internal organs; switching to the mirror technique will cause a different response because the internal organs are not symmetrically located. Therefore, the martial artist must be careful to apply the advanced techniques to the correct areas.

Techniques

In executing a Chin Na technique, the ultimate goal of the martial artist is to do the technique by feeling rather than by sight. By having a quick spontaneous reaction that is relatively independent of sight, the Chin Na technique will be done efficiently and smoothly. Thus, it is very important to always practice with a different number of partners to insure a wide range of response in a variety of circumstances.

The explanations for the techniques will be divided into two parts: application and type. The application part will describe the actual technique in detail. Again, the martial artist dressed in the black top will be referred to as "B," while the martial artist in the white will be "W." All the Chin Na will be done by and seen through the perspective of B. The martial artist in white will be the opponent or victim.

The type part will categorize the techniques into their respective classes. The last fifteen techniques are those of grasping the muscle, while most of the others are combination of types.

Type 1 = Misplacing the bone techniques
Type 2 = Dividing the muscle techniques

Technique 1
Figure 1: B folds any finger of W back and up the side. B's free hand must hold W's hand steady to keep W from twisting or escaping.

Type: 1. Finger joint is twisted unnaturally.

Figure 1

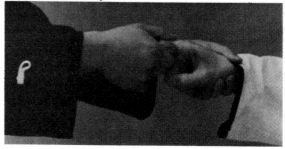

Technique 2
Figure 2: B twists W's thumb toward W while pushing the other fingers down.

Type: 1 and 2. Stretches the inside hand muscles and overextends finger joints.

Figure 2

Technique 3

Figure 3: B grabs any number of W's fingers and pushes them back and straight down to the floor. W must be forced down to his knees to prevent a counterattack.

Type: 1. Bends the finger joints.

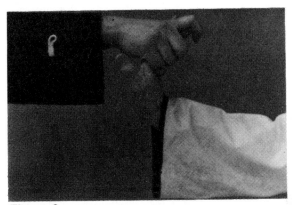

Figure 3

Technique 4

Figure 4: B with his left hand grabs W's wrist, and with his right puts his palm over the back of W's hand. B pushes the hand and forearm together as if trying to break a branch. To guard against a counterattack, B grabs W's right hand with his own right hand or vice versa—left to left. By grabbing the same hand, B is farther away from W's free hand.

Type: 1 and 2. Places stress on the joint and muscles of the wrist.

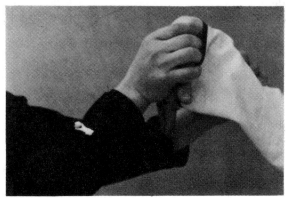

Figure 4

Technique 5

Figure 5:   W grabs B's wrist (right hand to right hand).

Figure 6:   With the left hand B pushes against W's hand; at the same time B moves his right hand up. By moving the hand up B is neutralizing W's power and preventing W from punching with his free hand.

Figure 7:   B moves his right hand over the wrist of W.

Figure 8:   B forces W down by applying pressure over the wrist. B must not let W's wrist turn over because the correct twisting position of W's wrist will then be lost. If W can make a complete turn, then B does not have proper control of the wrist. In addition, B sits Ssu Lieu Bu to avoid being hit by W's left hand.

Type: 2. When W's arm is put in position (fig. 6), the forearm muscles are put in an unnatural bend. By applying pressure over the wrist, pain is produced.

Figure 5

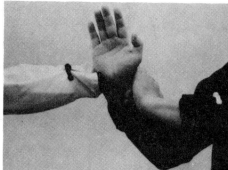

Figure 6

Figure 7

Figure 8

Technique 6

Figure 9:   W grabs B's wrist as in figure 5. B turns his right hand up and reaches under W's hand with his left. The left locks W's hand against B's right wrist.

Figure 10:   B forces W down by applying pressure over the wrist. B stands to the side of W to avoid a counterattack from W's left hand. B forces W all the way to the ground. If W can turn his hand, then B does not have the hand properly locked.

Type: 2. Same as technique 5.

Figure 9   Figure 10

Technique 7

Figure 11:   W grabs B's wrist as in figure 5. B turns the right hand clockwise so that the palm is facing up. At the same time, B's left hand grabs W's hand from underneath. Once this whole motion is complete, B slides his right hand up W's wrist.

Figure 12:   Once in position (fig. 11), B's right hand should push up on W's forearm while his left pushes up and twists (counterclockwise) W's wrist as far as possible. If W can spin and hit him, then B does not have the correct grip. B should raise W on his toes so that W cannot kick back.

Type: 2. By twisting and pushing up on the wrist the forearm muscles are hurt.

Figure 11

Figure12

Technique 8

Figure 13: This Chin Na is used as an attack. B must make the first move. B grabs W's wrist with his right hand using only the thumb and forefinger.

Figure 14: B puts his left palm against W's elbow.

Figure 15: B pushes up on W's wrist so that the back of W's hand is against B's palm. B should also press the area above the elbow to cause pain. B raises W on his toes so he cannot kick. B must not get too close to W's left hand to avoid being punched.

Type: 1 and 2. Muscles and joint of wrist are affected.

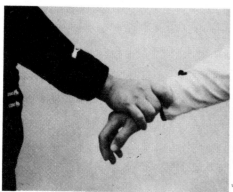

Figure 13

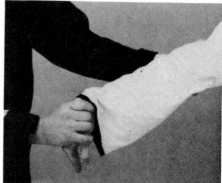

Figure 14

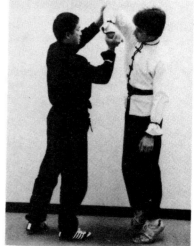

Figure 15

Technique 9

Figure 16: This Chin Na is used for attack. B grabs W's wrist with the right hand and the elbow with the left.

Figure 17: B forces W's hand inward while pushing downward on the wrist. At the same time B pulls W's whole arm toward himself. B sits Ssu Lieu Bu to avoid a counterattack from W's left hand. To cause more pain B squeezes the upper and lower arm together.

Type: 1 and 2. Muscles and joint of wrist are affected.

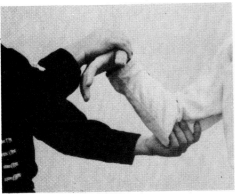

Figure 16

Figure 17

Technique 10

Figure 18: W grabs B's wrist as in figure 5. B moves to the outside while turning the right hand up clockwise to hook W's wrist. The left hand then goes to the area slightly above the elbow.

Figure 19: With the right hand, B pulls while the left hand presses down on the spot above the elbow. This technique can also be used as an attack; B must initially grab W's hand. B stands to the side to avoid W's left hand.

Type: 1. The elbow is forced to bend unnaturally.

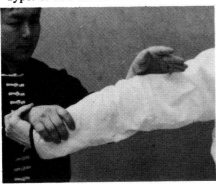

Figure 18

Figure 19

Technique 11

Figure 20: W grabs B as in figure 5. B moves the right hand up and over to hook the wrist of W. At the same time, B locks W's wrist by using the left hand moving over the top.

Figure 21: B pulls W's wrist up while pushing down on W's elbow with the armpit. B bends his left leg for added downward power and for added protection of his groin.

Type: 1 and 2. The muscles and joints of the wrist and elbow are simultaneously twisted and over extended.

Figure 20

Figure 21

Technique 12

Figure 22: This Chin Na is used for attack. B grabs W's right wrist using his right hand while moving his left arm under W's armpit.

Figure 23: B moves W's arm inward and locks both hands over W's wrist. B then pushes down on the back of W's right hand. B stands to the side of W to avoid a punch from W's left hand. In addition, B must raise W onto his toes to stop any kick from W's right leg.

Type: 1 and 2. The wrist joint and forearm muscles are affected.

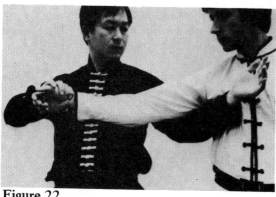

Figure 22

Figure 23

Technique 13

Figure 24: B grabs W's wrist with the right hand while grabbing the elbow with the left.

Figure 25: B holds W's elbow stationary while pushing the forearm back and the wrist down. To make this form easier B should step to W's side away from W's left hand. B's right leg should be hooked around W's left leg. B can make W fall by kicking out W's right leg.

Type: 1 and 2. Elbow and wrist joints misplaced.

Figure 24   Figure 25

Technique 14

Figure 26: As W punches, B blocks with the right hand and locks W's wrist against the blocking hand.

Figure 27: B grabs W's wrist with his left hand and turns W's hand so W's palm is facing inward.

Figure 28: B slides his right hand down and under W's tricep and hooks the muscle. At the same time B's left hand twists W's palm downward. From this position B can raise W's triceps while pulling down on the wrist. B stands to the side to avoid a counterattack from W's left arm.

Type: 1 and 2. The wrist, elbow, and shoulder and their muscles and joints are twisted and extended.

Figure 26   Figure 27

Figure 28

73

Technique 15

Figure 29: This Chin Na is used for attack. B grabs W's wrist with his right hand and places his left under W's elbow.

Figure 30: B slides his left hand to the elbow while pushing down on W's wrist.

Figure 31: B hooks his left hand around the side of W's upper arm while continuing to push down on W's wrist. The forearm should be as close to the upper arm as possible. B sits Ssu Lieu Bu to avoid being grabbed or hit by W's left arm.

Type: 1 and 2. The wrist and the muscles of the forearm are twisted.

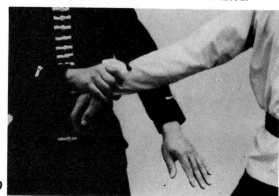

Figure 29

Figure 30

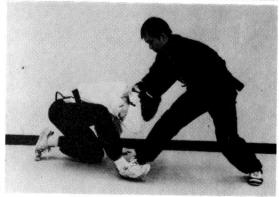

Figure 31

Technique 16

Figure 32:   This Chin Na is used for attack. B grabs W's wrist.

Figure 33:   B steps into W and raises W's arm while covering W's opposite arm and locking it. When W's hand is locked, W cannot reach over and punch or grab B. B's leg is behind W's.

Figure 34:   B brings W's arm down across his right shoulder so that W's palm is facing up and his elbow rests on B's shoulder. B pulls W's wrist down while raising him up. B raises W on his toes to keep W from kicking. B hooks his left leg around W's right leg.

Type: 1. Attacks elbow.

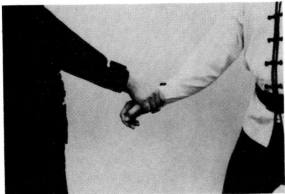

Figure 32

Figure 33

Figure 34

Technique 17

Figure 35: This Chin Na is used for attack. B grabs W's right wrist and lifts W's arm to chest level, while locking W's free hand with the left. When the hand is hooked, W is prevented from grabbing or punching. B must stand behind W.

Figure 36: B moves in so that his shoulder is under W's armpit. W's palm must point up in order to lock the elbow. To cause pain, B moves his shoulder up and W's hand down. B raises W on to his toes to prevent any kicks.

Type: 1. Misplaces elbow and shoulder.

Figure 35   Figure 36

Technique 18

Figure 37: This Chin Na is used for attack. B grabs W's right wrist with both hands and swings his body in front of W's. B must swing from the outside to the inside. B's shoulder is under W's armpit.

Figure 38: B pulls W's hand down. W's palm must be face up to lock in the elbow. B's left leg is in front of W's body. W must be raised on his toes to prevent any kick. W's arm must be pushed up to cause pain.

Type: 1. Attacks elbow.

Figure 37    Figure 38

Technique 19

Figure 39: This Chin Na is used for attack. B grabs W's wrist with his right hand and moves the left hand across W's waist to hook W's left hand. This prevents a counterattack from W's left hand.

Figure 40: B pulls W's arm tightly across his chest with W's elbow against B's chest. B then bends forward pulling up on W's right while pushing down on the arm with the shoulder. B's leg stands behind W.

Type: 1. Misplaces elbow.

Figure 39   Figure 40

Technique 20

Figure 41: This Chin Na is used for attack. This Chin Na is the same as Figures 39 and 40 except B's left hand pushes back and down on W's neck. B's arm must be above W's shoulder. B's leg stands behind W. B can make W fall down by kicking out his right leg.

Type: 1. Misplaces elbow.

Figure 41

Technique 21

Figure 42: As W punches, B blocks with his left hand and steps forward with the right leg while hooking W's arm with his right. B has formed two White Crane Wings. This Chin Na can be used for straight or circular punches.

Figure 43: B's right arm reaches over to grab W's right wrist while his left pushes the arm back and down. B stands to the side of W to avoid W's left arm. W must be raised on his toes to keep him from kicking.

Type: 1 and 2. Upper arm muscles are twisted and elbow is twisted.

Figure 42   Figure 43

Technique 22

Figure 44: W grabs B's wrist as in figure 5. B grabs W's right hand with his left and throws his right elbow forward while turning B's right wrist down. As B swings his elbow forward, he may hit W in the face with it.

Figure 45: B swings his elbow completely over W's arm. Once B's arm is completely over he pushes back and up with it, at the same time twisting W's wrist downward. B stands to the side to avoid W's left hand. Again, W must be raised to his toes to keep him from kicking.

Type: 1 and 2. Upper arm muscles are twisted and the elbow and wrist joint are misplaced.

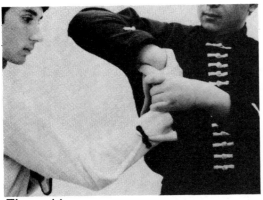

Figure 44

Figure 45

Technique 23

Figure 46: W grabs B's wrist as in figure 5. B turns his right palm out in a counterclockwise motion and grabs W's wrist with his left hand.

Figure 47: Twisting his right hand out of W's grab, B grabs W's wrist with his right hand. Both of B's hands then push on the back of W's hand while pulling the whole arm downward. B sits Ssu Lieu Bu to avoid W's left hand.

Type: 1 and 2. Over-extends and misplaces wrist muscles and joint.

Figure 46

Figure 47

Technique 24

Figure 48: W uses his right hand to grab the inside wrist of B.

Figure 49: B grabs W's wrist with his left hand while turning his right elbow toward W.

Figure 50: B completely brings his elbow over W's arm and pushes back with it against W's elbow. At the same time, B twists W's wrist downward. B stands to the side to avoid counterattack.

Type: 1 and 2. Misplaces wrist and twists forearm muscles.

Figure 48

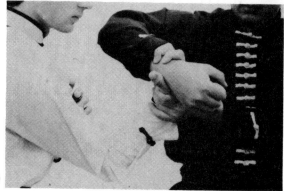

Figure 49

Figure 50

Technique 25

Figure 51:   W uses his right hand to grab B's wrist from the inside.

Figure 52:   B steps to the side, with his left leg in front, and places his left hand under W's wrist.

Figure 53:   B pulls W's arm over his shoulder while turning W's wrist clockwise. B raises W off his feet to avoid counterattack.

Type: 1 and 2. The upper arm muscles are twisted while shoulder joint is misplaced.

Figure 51

Figure 52

Figure 53

Technique 26

Figure 54: This Chin Na is used for attack. B uses his right hand to grab W's wrist from the inside.

Figure 55: B slides his left arm under W's elbow and reaches over with it to grab his own right hand. B then pushes up with his left arm while pushing down with both his hands on W's wrist. B stands to W's right side to avoid a counterattack from W's left hand. B raises W off his toes so that W cannot kick.

Type: 1. Misplaces elbow.

Figure 54

Figure 55

Technique 27

Figure 56: B can use this as an attack or while shaking hands.

Figure 57: B slides his left arm under W's right arm while turning W's right palm up. As B's left hand reaches W, he locks it against the neck and pushes down on W's hand. W's elbow must be locked on B's left arm. B stands slightly to the side and raises W off his feet so that W cannot counterattack.

Type: 1. Misplaces elbow.

Figure 56

Figure 57

82

Technique 28

Figure 58: W's left hand grabs B's right wrist.

Figure 59: B locks W's palm against his wrist while the right hand moves up and to the side of W's wrist.

Figure 60: B moves his hand over W's wrist.

Figure 61: B pushes straight down on W's wrist. If W can turn his body clockwise and strike B with his right hand, then B is not properly controlling the correct muscle (the muscles between the fourth and fifth finger). If done properly, W should be forced down in front of B. B sits back to avoid a counterattack from W's left hand.

Type: 2. Twists wrist and finger muscles.

Figure 58

Figure 59

Figure 60

Figure 61

Technique 29

Figure 62:   W grabs B's wrist as in figure 58. With his left hand, B locks W's wrist while moving his right hand up so that W's wrist is between B's thumb and fingers.

Figure 63:   B starts to swing his right elbow over W's arm.

Figure 64:   B moves his arm over W's elbow until B's armpit is over it. B then pushes down on W's wrist and elbow. B's right hand grabs W's wrist for more power and leverage. This technique can be used to dislocate W's arm if B uses a quick jerking power in this step. B is kneeling to the side of W to avoid counterattack.

Type: 1 and 2. Twists wrist muscles and misplaces elbow.

Figure 62

Figure 63

Figure 64

Technique 30

Figure 65: W grabs B's wrist as in figure 58. B turns his palm up while taking hold of W's hand from underneath.

Figure 66: B turns his right hand onto W's wrist.

Figure 67: B holds W's wrist secure while pushing W's whole arm from right to left. As B pushes he should assume a low posture to prevent W from spinning around, escaping, or striking with his right hand.

Type: 2. Twists muscles running through wrist.

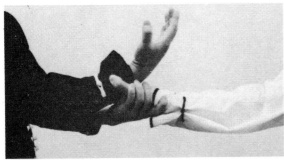

Figure 65

Figure 66

Figure 67

Technique 31

Figure 68:   W grabs the upper part of B's right arm and chest. This hold is popularly used in Judo. This Chin Na and Technique 43 can effectively counteract this hold.

Figure 69:   B with his left hand reaches under his own right arm and locks W's left hand. At the same time B uses his right hand to reach over W's left arm.

Figure 70:   B turns W's wrist down while pushing W's elbow from right to left. B is to the side of W to avoid being kicked or punched.

Type: 1 and 2. Misplaces elbow and twists wrist muscles.

Figure 68

Figure 69

Figure 70

Technique 32

Figure 71: This is an attack and therefore must be done quickly. B, using his right hand, grabs W's left wrist.

Figure 72: B slides his left hand under W's forearm. In this Chin Na, B must keep moving toward the left side of W. This prevents W from striking with his right hand.

Figure 73: B pushes W's wrist towards W's body while hooking his own left hand on W's upper arm.

Figure 74: B pushes down on W's arm while twisting W's wrist and stepping forward with his right leg. B is standing to the side and back of W.

Type: 1 and 2. Stress is put on shoulder joint and wrist muscles.

Figure 71

Figure 72

Figure 73

Figure 74

Technique 33

Figure 75: W's left hand grabs B's right wrist.

Figure 76: B raises his hand while locking W's wrist.

Figure 77: B slides his elbow over W's arm and then pushes down on it while twisting W's wrist. W should not be allowed to turn over or twist his left arm. If B allows this, W can turn clockwise and strike B. B stands to the side of W.

Type: 2. Pressure is put on the elbow joint and the wrist is twisted.

Figure 75

Figure 76

Figure 77

Technique 34

Figure 78: B, using his right hand, grabs W's right wrist while he pushes W's elbow with the other hand. The hand on the elbow prevents W from striking.

Figure 79: B steps into W and puts his left hand behind W's head (or grabs his hair) while his right locks the jaw at the chin. B then jerks W's head back and to the side using both hands. In order to break W's neck a jerking power is applied 45 degrees upward. B stands behind W.

Type: 1. Dislocates neck.

Figure 78   Figure 79

Technique 35

Figure 80: W punches and B blocks with his right hand.

Figure 81: B steps forward and grabs W's hair. B then pulls W to the ground. This Chin Na is not used so much for controlling but for forcing an opponent to the ground where other techniques may be used.

Type: 1. Puts stress on neck and wrist.

Figure 80   Figure 81

Technique 36

Figure 82: As W attempts to cut B with the left hand, B grabs W's hand. B's palm is covering the back of W's hand.

Figure 83: B pulls W's hand down. When B performs this Chin Na he must be careful of W's right hand since it is free to punch.

Figure 84: B raises W's hand straight up to the center of the back. B must twist W's fingers and exert enough pressure upwards so that W is on his toes. Once on his toes W cannot kick. B must stand to the side to avoid being punched by W's right hand.

Type: 1 and 2. Twists muscles and joints of wrist and fingers.

Figure 82

Figure 83

Figure 84

Technique 37

Figure 85: W with his right hand grabs B's right hand.

Figure 86: B steps to his left while turning his own right palm up. Simultaneously, B must lock W's right hand by using his left.

Figure 87: B steps forward and to the side with his right leg. At no time should B turn his back directly in front of W. If B turns in front, W can pull on B's arm and make B fall.

Figure 88: B turns 180 degrees counterclockwise while moving his right hand over W's wrist. As B turns, W's arm swings over B's head.

Figure 89: B swings W's arm down and up while twisting the wrist. B should twist W's wrist to the extent that W is forced on his toes—thus losing the ability to kick. This same Chin Na can be used left hand to left hand.

Type: 2. Wrist is twisted.

Figure 85   Figure 86   Figure 87

Figure 89

Technique 38

Figure 90:   W grabs B as in figure 85. B steps back with his right leg while moving his own right hand up (palm down). At the same time B locks W's right hand with his left from underneath.

Figure 91:   B turns 180 degrees clockwise while swinging W's arm up. B is in the incorrect position if he turns his back directly in front of W.

Figure 92:   B moves W's arm across his own head while also pulling down on W's arm to make W fall.

Type: 1 and 2. Elbow and wrist are twisted.

Figure 90

Figure 91

Figure 92

Technique 39

Figure 93: This Chin Na is used to control an opponent from the rear. B grabs W's fingers on the inside.

Figure 94: B lifts up W's hand while swinging his own elbow over W's arm. W's arm must be straight.

Figure 95: B turns W's wrist toward W's forearm while also pushing down on W's elbow with the right arm. B's left knee touches the ground to avoid a counterattack to the groin.

Type: 1 and 2. Overextends the elbow and twists the wrist.

Figure 93

Figure 94

Figure 95

Technique 40

Figure 96: B grasps W's fingers as in figure 93, except B's arm is on the inside. This technique is used to control an opponent from the rear. B must hold W's elbow to prevent him from striking back.

Figure 97: B lifts up W's hand and then pushes down on W's fingers. B's left hand is used to help control W's arm. W is lifted onto his toes to keep him from kicking.

Type: 2. Twists wrist and palm muscles.

Figure 96   Figure 97

Technique 41

Figure 98: B grabs W's right hand from the back.

Figure 99: With both hands, B twists W's wrist to the outside. To bring W to the floor B will also pull W's arm toward himself. While B is performing this Chin Na he must be careful of W's free left hand; therefore, B sits back slightly.

Type: 2. Twists wrist.

Figure 98   Figure 99

Technique 42

Figure 100: B uses his right hand to grab W's right hand. W may be doing anything—from starting a punch to blocking.

Figure 101: B steps in back of W and hooks W's left arm with his own left.

Figure 102: B slides his right arm under W's arm and then hooks both hands over W's neck; B then applies downward pressure. When B controls W he should have either his right or left leg forward to prevent W from kicking backwards.

Type: 1. Neck is extended.

Figure 100

Figure 101

Figure 102

Technique 43

Figure 103: This Chin Na technique is known as "the child worshipping the Buddha." W grabs B's shirt.

Figure 104: B with both his hands grabs W's hand and turns it 90 degrees.

Figure 105: B applies pressure over the wrist while bending his upper body. If W can twist his wrist then B does not have proper control.

Type: 2. Wrist muscles are twisted.

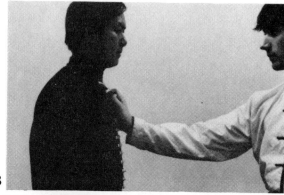

Figure 103

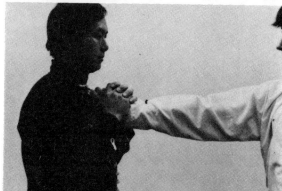

Figure 104

Figure 105

Technique 44

Figure 106: W grabs B's right shoulder with his right hand.

Figure 107: B reaches over with his left hand and locks W's right hand onto the shoulder. B at the same time swings his right elbow over W's arm.

Figure 108: B applies downward pressure on W's arm. B must watch that W does not grab his leg as he is forced down.

Type: 1 and 2. Elbow joint and wrist are twisted.

Figure 106 　　　　　Figure 107

Figure 108

Technique 45

Figure 109: W grabs B's right shoulder with his left hand.

Figure 110: B reaches over with his left hand and locks W's left hand onto the shoulder. At the same time, B swings his right arm up.

Figure 111: B continues to swing his right arm until it encircles W's arm. B then locks both of his hands together and lifts up. B can dislocate W's elbow by a quick jerk at this step. B must get W turned to the side by lifting up on W's elbow. This keeps W from counterattacking.

Type: 1. Elbow is turned and twisted.

Figure 109

Figure 110

Figure 111

Technique 46

Figure 112: W, using his right hand, grabs B's left shoulder.

Figure 113: With his right hand, B locks W's hand onto the shoulder. At the same time B swings his left arm over W's shoulder. B must not let W turn his right wrist. If W turns his wrist, B cannot control him.

Figure 114: B then applies pressure over W's forearm to force him down.

Type: 2. Wrist muscles are twisted.

Figure 112

Figure 113

Figure 114

Technique 47

Figure 115: This Chin Na is applied anytime a martial artist has his lead leg pointing directly forward. B slides his right leg behind W's lead leg.

Figure 116: B forces his knee into W's knee until W is down.

Type: 1. Knee is bent.

Figure 115

Figure 116

Technique 48

Figure 117: This Chin Na is used anytime an opponent has his feet parallel. B slides his left leg behind W's lead leg.

Figure 118: B pushes his knee into W's calf until W is forced down.

Type: 2. Knee is bent.

Figure 117

Figure 118

Technique 49

Figure 119: As W kicks, B steps to the side and catches W's leg from underneath.

Figure 120: B locks both hands over W's instep and then applies pressure down on the foot. B must not stand too close to W, or W will be able to punch him.

Type: 2. Ankle is twisted.

Figure 119   Figure 120

Technique 50

Figure 121: W grabs B at the small of the back using the right hand.

Figure 122: B turns counterclockwise and swings his left arm over W's elbow. B then locks his own arm against W's elbow.

Figure 123: B applies force on W's arm (above the elbow) while B's right hand reaches around to grab hold of W's right hand. B forces W down.

Type: 2. Elbow joint is bent.

Figure 121

Figure 122

Figure 123

Technique 51

Figure 124: W grabs B's collar with his right hand.

Figure 125: B turns clockwise while locking W's hand on the collar. At the same time, B lifts his right elbow above W's right elbow.

Figure 126: B uses his right arm to apply pressure down over W's forearm and elbow.

Type: 1 and 2. Elbow joint is bent and wrist is twisted.

Figure 124

Figure 125

Figure 126

Technique 52

Figure 127: B grabs the side of W's jaw, turns his fingers up and then pulls down. This Chin Na dislocates the hinge of the jaw. B must do this quickly before W can punch or kick.

Type: 1. Dislocates jaw.

Figure 127

Technique 53

Figure 128: B steps to the side of W and hooks his fingers on the back side of the windpipe. If the fingers can meet in the back of the windpipe, then the person will die of suffocation because a piece of cartilage will be forced over the larynx. B puts his left hand around W's neck so W cannot move his head away.

Type: 1. Throat is cut off.

Figure 128

Technique 54

Figure 129: B grabs W around the lower back and pulls inward while his chin and chest press forward. B must do this quickly before W can punch.

Type: 1 and 2. The spinal column and the muscles along the waist are injured.

Figure 129

Technique 55

Figure 130: W, who is on the ground, attempts to kick B. B grabs the leg and twists the ankle inwards. B can sit on the leg once he catches it.

Type: 1. Twists ankle.

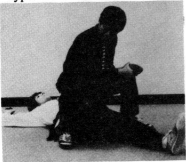

Figure 130

Technique 56

Figure 131: B quickly drops in front of W and hooks his right foot around W's ankle. With the left foot B kicks W's knee to disrupt W's knee joint.

Type: 1. Disrupts knee joint.

Figure 131

From Technique 57 until Technique 71, the pictures will show the methods and areas of grasping the muscle. Refer to Chapter 2 for a detailed explanation.

Technique 57

Figure 132: While B's left hand holds W's right hand to keep it steady and from escaping, B squeezes the tip of W's fingers. Any finger may be squeezed.

Figure 132

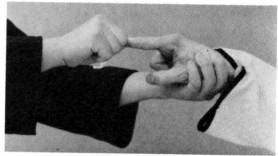

Technique 58

Figure 133: B squeezes the knuckle of his thumb into the area between the tendons that lead into the fingers.

Figure 133

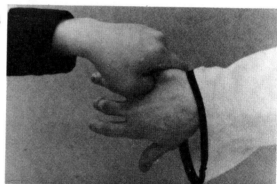

Technique 59

Figure 134: B holds W's hand while his fingers penetrate into the pit between the thumb and forefinger.

Figure 134

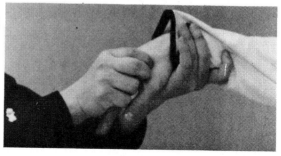

Technique 60

Figure 135: While holding and bending W's left wrist, B grabs the top muscle of the upper forearm. This will make the hand numb. B must stand to the side to avoid a counterattack.

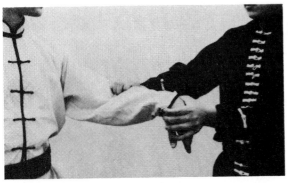

Figure 135

Technique 61

Figure 136: While holding W's elbow, B grasps the area slightly above the elbow joint. This will make the arm numb. B stands to the side to avoid being punched with W's left hand.

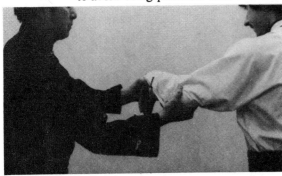

Figure 136

Technique 62

Figure 137: B pinches his fingers into W's deltoid muscle slightly in front of the shoulder joint. This will make the shoulder area numb. B must be careful of W's left arm.

Figure 137

Technique 63

Figure 138: B grasps the upper part of the triceps. This will make the arm numb. B stands behind W to avoid counterattack from W's free hand.

Figure 138

Technique 64

Figure 139: B grasps the muscle in front of the armpit. This will numb the shoulder area. If enough power is used, the person may become unconscious because of the pain and contraction of the muscles around the lung.

Figure 139

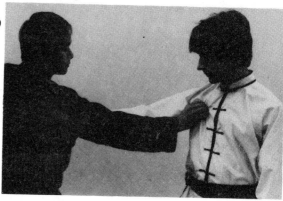

Technique 65

Figure 140: B grasps the muscle in back of the armpit to make the shoulder area numb.

Figure 140

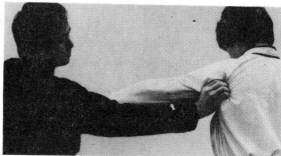

Technique 66

Figure 141: B pinches the big muscles running to the side and back of the neck. May cause unconsciousness by sending pain into the brain.

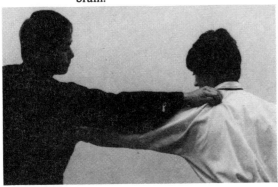

Figure 141

Technique 67

Figure 142: B grasps the muscle on the back of W's neck. B must stand to the side to avoid W's right hand.

Figure 142

Technique 68

Figure 143: B pinches the neck muscle slightly behind the throat. B must pinch and pull while watching W's left hand.

Figure 143

Technique 69

Figure 144: B grabs the side of the waist under the ribs to cause extreme pain. B must stand to the side to avoid W's left hand.

Figure 144

Technique 70

Figure 145: As W punches, B slides to the side and grabs the area above the knee, causing pain to the leg.

Figure 145

Technique 71

Figure 146: As W kicks, B blocks the leg and grasps the areas on either side of the shin near the center numbing the leg. B must be careful to avoid being punched by W.

Figure 146

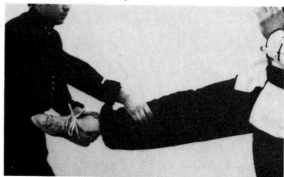

Treatment of Injuries from Fundamental Chin Na

While practicing the fundamental techniques of Chin Na it is possible to receive various types of injuries. Through experience, these injuries can be divided into several groups. The injuries that a student receives during Chin Na practice can be cured if the proper procedures are followed. Administering first aid to oneself and others is an important aspect of any martial art.

In general, the first type of aid to be usually administered is massage and then herbal treatments. For a review on massage, refer back to Chapter 4. Herbs, like massage, are a common way to cure various injuries. In China, an herb is not necessarily a medicine derived from a plant. An herb can be anything of medicinal value which has been taken from animals, insects, minerals, etc. Most herbs reflect the properties of their environment; an herbal plant living in a cool moving stream will display properties of coldness. Most Chinese herbs are mixtures of several elements.

Herbs are usually used either for external use or internal use. Herbs which are used on the outer or external portions of the body usually are meant to help cure bruises, cuts, sore spots, inflammation, and other disorders. The herbs which are used for external purposes can come in the form of ointments, liquids, alcohol suspensions, and powders.

Herbs that are used for internal purposes have as their goal the curing of more serious disorders such as ulcers, fevers, heart troubles and internal bleeding; for this reason, internal herbs must be taken into the body directly. For the martial artist the use of internal herbs is very important. First, to get rid of bruises which are deep in the body, ingested herbs are necessary, because the techniques of massage are not effective on very deep bruises. Second, many internally taken herbs such as ginseng help the circulation of Chi. Herbs that help the circulation of Chi assist a martial artist in recovering from bruises which hinder his Chi circulation.

Because the types and kinds of herbs are too numerous to list, it is a good policy for the martial artist to find a good Chinese herbal store. The owners of these stores are usually experienced herbalists who can prescribe the correct remedy. Many good herb stores are located in big cities where people of Chinese ancestry live.

The first type of injury which can occur in the practice of Chin Na is to the muscle. Because many fundamental Chin Na techniques require the twisting, grasping, and pulling of muscles, it is quite easy for muscles to receive some sort of injury. In this case, the injured spot is usually soft to the touch because lymph and some blood have accumulated around the injured section. With injured muscles, the best remedy is to massage the hurt area. Massage helps the healing to occur faster. Later, an herb can be used.

The next type of injury which may occur is a bruise. A bruised area, unlike that of an injured muscle, is hard to the touch because it has a high concentration of dead blood cells. Also, the pain from a bruise is localized in a very sensitive area. Most bruises can be located by the discoloration of the skin. To get rid of a bruise, the most effective method is to use herbs in conjunction with massage.

The third type of injury common to the practice of Chin Na is to the ligaments. Injury to the ligaments can especially occur in misplacing the bone Chin Na because its whole purpose is to unhinge the bones at their joints. When unhinging occurs, the ligaments are overstretched. With this sort of injury, it is best to use herbal treatment with rest. In time the ligaments will return to their normal state. Massaging a ligament is not good because this will irritate or stretch it out even further.

The fourth type of injury, dislocation, can result in serious problems if it is not attended to immediately. With any dislocation the first priority is to relocate the joint. Usually, the areas most likely to get dislocated are fingers, hand, elbow, shoulder, and knee. Each one will be treated separately.

Relocating a finger can usually be accomplished by the practitioner himself, but it is better for someone else to do it. To relocate the finger, first place it between the fore and index finger of the good hand, or between those of a partner. Once the dislocated finger is firmly held in place, pull with a constant motion and bend the finger in. The pulling and bending will slip the finger back into place. This process is shown in figures 147 and 148.

The second common area that may be dislocated is the hand. This type of dislocation usually occurs when the hand receives a sharp blow—the bones which make up the wrist area may pop out. To relocate the bone, the person performing the relocation must lock one of his hands with that of the dislocated hand. With a constant motion the person doing the relocation

Figure 147

Figure 148

112

pulls the hand straight out while pushing the bone into place with the help of grease (fig. 149). By pulling out the hand, the bone can fit into its slot much more easily. This relocation process must be done on some flat surface.

A third joint which can be dislocated during Chin Na practice is the elbow. Usually another person is needed to help relocate the elbow. First, one hand is placed under the dislocated elbow while the other hand grabs the wrist (fig. 150). Once secured, the dislocated arm is pulled straight out with the palm facing up. The hand under the elbow must remain firmly set. When the arm is pulled out, bend the forearm up toward the body as in figure 151. By pulling the arm straight out, the joint is aligned properly. Once the forearm is bent up, the joint becomes set into place. This same method is applied when the knee becomes dislocated; the leg is pulled, and the calf is bent toward the body. The methods for the knee and elbow are similar because the joints have the same basic structure.

Figure 149

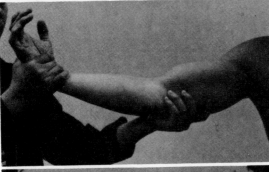

Figure 150

Figure 151

The last serious dislocation which can occur is at the shoulder joint. For this type it is best to have two people relocate the shoulder, but this is not absolutely necessary. First, the dislocated arm is pulled outward and parallel to the ground; this aligns the dislocated bone (fig. 152). While one person is pulling, the other holds the injured person tightly around the chest. With a constant motion, the person holding the arm moves it across the chest of the injured person as in figure 153; this movement puts the joint into place.

After any dislocated joint is put back into place, herbal treatments should be applied around the joint to stop inflammation. The person who dislocated an elbow, shoulder, or knee should not engage in any violent activity until the injured area is returned to normal functioning.

A broken bone, the last kind of serious injury, usually should not be handled by the student. The person with a broken bone should see a doctor immediately. If no doctor is around within miles, then the broken area must be set and made immovable until a doctor can be seen. Waiting too long to reset the bone will cause bruises to accumulate. In addition, there is a possibility of the bone setting itself into a painful position. Setting the bone requires that the broken part be realigned into its original position. This is done by pulling out and slowly reconnecting the bone like two jigsaw pieces. Once the bone is set, it is made immovable so that the broken part, while repairing itself, will reset into its original position. However, many times

Figure 152

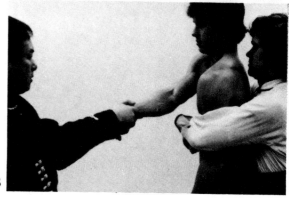

Figure 153

only a crack in the bone will occur. In these cases seeing a doctor is not absolutely necessary. Instead, the person should avoid violent contact to the injured area. Cracked bones will usually heal themselves in time. With cracked bones no massage should be done—this will only irritate the injury.

Advanced Chin Na

Sealing the Breath or Vein

Sealing the breath or vein, unlike cavity press, is only somewhat related to the circulation of Chi. The effectiveness of a cavity strike is limited to its time relationship with Chi. But in sealing the breath or vein the correspondence is not that great. For example, the windpipe may be broken at any time. But there are certain times when sealing the breath or vein can be most effective.

Second, cavity press techniques allow for more killing methods than sealing the breath or vein; in cavity press it is very easy, once the techniques are mastered, to kill a person. But with sealing the breath or vein the general purpose is to render a person unconscious and later revive them. Of course, if the person is not revived, they may die in certain cases.

Third, cavity press methods must be more precise than those of sealing the breath or vein. To strike a cavity the attack must be extremely accurate. In contrast, sealing the breath or vein does not require the precision of cavity press; the desired target for sealing the breath or vein is not a point, but an area. For this reason, the penetration of power in cavity press Chin Na must be to the right depth. On the other hand, the penetrating power needed to make sealing the breath or vein effective is not as sharp, so long as the general vicinity of the target area gets the power. Again, as a result, the hand forms of cavity press are designed to pinpoint power while those of sealing the breath or vein are to collapse a certain portion of the body. Thus the power must be spread over a wide area.

Technique 1 (fig. 154)

Sealing the vein: The arm is wrapped around the neck. The neck is then squeezed by the arm and side of the waist. The pressure from the arms and waist will shut off the blood to the brain.

Figure 154

Technique 2 (fig. 155)

Sealing the vein: Both sides of the neck are simultaneously struck by the sides of the palm. The power must penetrate to the level of the veins and arteries to close them. The power of the attack will cause the muscles and nerves of the neck to contract and thus cut off blood to the brain.

Figure 155

Technique 3 (fig. 156)

Sealing the breath and vein: This technique combines both aspects of sealing the breath and sealing the vein. The right arm is around the neck while the left hand is over the back of the head. As the right arm pulls in squeezing the throat and side of the neck, the left hand pushes the head forward. Thus, no air can enter the lungs or blood reach the brain.

Figure 156

Technique 4 (fig. 157)

Sealing the breath: The right hand is wrapped around the windpipe while the left hand holds the back of the neck or head to keep the victim from escaping. The right hand keeps applying pressure until the fingers meet behind the windpipe. When the fingers meet, a bone from the windpipe is forced over the air passage, thus cutting off the oxygen supply.

Figure 157

Technique 5 (fig. 158)

Sealing the breath: As a punch is blocked, or as the arm is grabbed, B steps into W and strikes the area of the shoulder blade with the forearm. The power will force all the muscles in that area to violently contract around the lung, thus stopping the breathing process.

Figure 158

Technique 6 (fig. 159)

Sealing the breath: The same as the previous technique except the front chest muscles are made to violently contract around the lungs.

Figure 159

Technique 7 (fig. 160)

Sealing the breath: This is essentially the same as figure 158 except the palm is used to strike the back area.

Figure 160

Technique 8 (fig. 161)

Sealing the breath: This technique is related to figure 159, but only now the palm is used to strike the muscle. The results are the same as those in Technique 6.

Figure 161

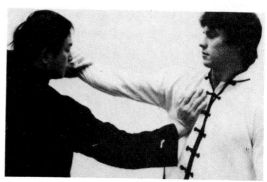

Technique 9 (fig. 162)

Sealing the breath: B uses his palm to strike the area around W's solar plexus. The shock to this area will cause both lungs to violently contract; thus, no air can enter the lungs.

Figure 162

Technique 10 (fig. 163)

Sealing the breath: B uses a palm to strike W's waist. The power will force the muscles to violently contract around the internal organs. The pain from the organs and the restricted function of the diaphragm will cause the person to faint.

Figure 163

Theory of Cavity Press

Cavity press Chin Na is considered a high skill in Chinese Wu Su. The mastery of cavity press requires a wide range of knowledge and skills; it requires everything from advanced traditional medical expertise to extremely powerful hands. Because the advanced cavity press techniques require internal power, the whole process of training will take many years. For this reason, internal styles such as Tai Chi will usually specialize in some sort of cavity press.

The purpose of cavity press Chin Na is usually for control, but many techniques can kill. More specifically, there are four general methods used to control a person; to make a certain part of the body numb, to make a person faint, to make a person lose his voice, and to make a person die. The four types of cavity press are: striking the cavity, striking the Chi, striking the blood, and striking the yin yang. The martial artist who practices cavity press must be very careful because hitting a cavity may produce a variety of effects—anything from slight pain to death.

Out of about 700 cavities used in acupuncture (some books on acupuncture list 350 cavities because they count only cavities on one side of the body), the martial artist practicing cavity press will use roughly 108 cavities: 72 cavities which can cause local paralysis, fainting, or loss of voice, and 36 which can cause death. The physical effect of an attack on one of the 108 cavities will depend on such things as the season of the year and time of day.

Because the human body follows natural cycles, the circulation of Chi will likewise follow certain set patterns or cycles. Thus, during certain times of the Chi cycle, the cavities will vary in their sensitivity to different kinds of stimulation. The martial artist must therefore have expert knowledge of Chi cycles and cavities, and their response to stimulation.

Striking the cavity, the first type of cavity press, involves attacking the nerve under a cavity to cause local paralysis. The sudden shock to the nerve running through the cavity will disrupt the local area and cause paralysis. Once a certain part of the body loses its function, the martial artist can easily control his opponent. Attacking the funny bone to cause paralysis is an example of this kind of cavity press.

The second type of cavity press is striking the Chi. It involves attacking the nervous system, and thus the Chi, that runs through a cavity. By attacking the nervous system, stagnation of Chi occurs. Once the Chi circulation is stopped, and paralysis begins, the person can either feel numb in a certain area, faint, or die. In this type of cavity press the person may not die immediately; instead, the victim will die once the Chi reaches the cavity where it can go no further. This point of Chi stagnation will adversely affect the victim's health since the proper flow of Chi is necessary for life.

The third type of cavity press is striking the blood. This type, in contrast to striking the Chi, which affects the nervous system, attacks the internal organs by direct or indirect means. An example of a direct attack on an internal organ would be a strike to the liver using internal power; such an attack would not stop on the surface of the body, but penetrate a few inches into the liver. When such a blow occurs the liver can literally explode and lose all its functions. An indirect attack would harm an internal organ by rupturing something around an organ. For example, by striking the temple a martial artist could break the arteries and veins in that area. The broken arteries and veins would then cause damage to the brain.

The last type of cavity press is called striking the yin yang and entails hitting spots where the body's energy changes from yin (negative) to yang (positive) or from yang to yin. Traditional Chinese medical doctors believe that as the Chi circulates through the body it takes on the aspects of yin or yang, and will cyclically change from yin to yang and vice versa. The moments that the Chi changes are very vulnerable ones for human beings. If the point of exchange is violently disrupted, then the person can die. To properly master this type, the martial artist should know the times and points that the Chi changes its yin or yang aspects.

In all types of the cavity press there are four general areas that are attacked. Each area when it is struck will produce a variety of symptoms depending on the extent, depth, and location of the attacking power. The first area of common attack is the head. The head, or brain, can be hurt directly or through cavities; the usual method is to strike it directly. The severity of attack may result in anything from a mild concussion to death. Any time the head is struck with force several symptons will show the extent of injury: vomiting, slow pulse, weak breath, inactive eyes, and paleness.

The second common area of attack is the spine. The spine is usually attacked through cavities because it is well protected by bone. Because the spine is actively important to health on a constant basis, it may be attacked independently of the Chi cycles that flow through it. Many effects of an attack are immediate, while some effects may take time to develop. When the spine is struck, two general things may occur; first, the spine itself may lose all function; second, the functioning of the four limbs may be damaged. The symptoms of spinal injury are a pale face, irregular breath, irregular heart beat, numbness in the limbs, and inability to urinate.

The third place of attack is directed toward the cavities. The cavities may be roughly divided into those that are sensitive and those that are insensitive. When a sensitive cavity is struck the effect that is produced is immediate and violent; striking the solar plexus (a cavity) is an example. When the solar plexus is hit with great force the heart will go into an immediate convulsion. When the insensitive cavities are struck with sufficient force, the effect will take time to reveal itself since the insensitive cavities are usually related to the circulation of chi.

The fourth area of attack is the internal organs. The organs are usually attacked directly and their symptoms will depend on the particular function of each organ. Because there are several organs that can be attacked, the symptoms for damage will not be listed. The easiest and weakest organ for attack is the liver because of its soft nature. The second easiest to attack is the spleen. After the spleen, the kidney, stomach, intestines, lung, and bladder can be attacked. The kidneys are the easiest to attack and the bladder is the hardest. (The brain may also be included in this list.)

Training Methods for Cavity Press

The training methods for the mastery of cavity press Chin Na are extremely difficult because it takes years to practice and master all the different complexities. All the original theory for the training methods were derived from the *I Ching* which was written over 5,000 years ago. The *I Ching* first formulated the principles of the yin/yang cycle and Pau Kua.

The theory to be found in the *I Ching* is too complex and not readily explainable; therefore, this book will simply describe the more easily available features of cavity press.

In mastering cavity press Chin Na, the martial artist must develop either internal power or forceful penetrating external power. The development of internal power requires at least ten years of training under a qualified master; for this reason it will be beyond the scope of this chapter to describe the methods. Although the development of internal power cannot be described in this chapter, the development of a forceful and strong external power can be described.

The first step in building up power for cavity press is to strengthen the hand and fingers for striking. When a person starts to train for cavity press Chin Na, he can use a variety of striking forms. The martial artist can use a fist, palm, various kicks, elbow, knee, bottom of palm, or even grasping forms. But because cavities are small areas, the best way to approach or attack them is by a small form, attack forms that can concentrate external power to a fine point. As a result, the common method of attacking a cavity is by using one or two outstretched fingers, or the knuckles of the index and forefinger. But to effectively use a single finger in attacking a cavity, the finger's strength and durability must be increased.

There are roughly five steps in building up the fingers for cavity press Chin Na. The first step is to perform push ups on the fingers until the exercise can be done with ease. The martial artist should then gradually use fewer fingers until he can do complete push ups by using only the forefinger. Once this is accomplished, the martial artist should practice bouncing his weight off the forefinger while in the push up position.

Next, the martial artist should obtain some Chinese green beans and poke his hands in them to make the skin on the fingers tough. The Chinese green beans are used because they act as a sort of herb and calm the burning sensation of the skin. After practicing with the green beans, the martial artist must massage his hands in hot water to help eliminate bruises caused by poking the green beans.

The next stage is to poke the fingers into sand. The purpose of this is to further toughen the skin and fingers. Sand taken from a beach is adequate for this step. Again, the martial artist should massage his hands in hot water to help eliminate bruises.

The final stage is to poke the fingers into iron filings; the hard filings will make the skin and fingers extremely tough. This stage will require the use of a simple herb wine (which can be obtained at a Chinese herb store) to help, along with massage, eliminate the internal bruises that developed while poking the hands in the iron filings.

Looking over the training method that develops the strength and hardness of the fingers, it is easy to see that a martial artist who has great external penetration power and a knowledge of cavities can easily kill a person using only one finger. The finger, because of extensive training, is like a thin steel rod moving at a high rate of speed; once the finger hits its mark, it can cause extreme damage. Once a person understands the long training that is needed for this special skill, the seemingly fantastic stories of martial artists using one finger to overcome an opponent become more real and less fantastic.

Once the fingers and hands are built up, the martial artist requires four things to make cavity press Chin Na effective: concentration, impulse power, penetration, and accuracy. Concentration is trained by lighting an incense stick or candle and watching it steadily for at least five minutes without being distracted by stray thoughts. While concentrating, the mind must not only remain focused at every moment, but it must also remain relaxed.

Impulse and penetration power may both be trained together using a candle or sand. If a candle is used the martial artist should light it and attempt to put out the flame by punching at it. The punching hand, as it comes forward cannot touch the flame. Once the flame can be easily put out, the martial artist should step farther away from the candle and once again attempt to put out the flame. The further away the student can stand, the greater will be the penetration and impulse power.

The second way to practice penetration and impulse power is to punch a heavy piece of cotton which has been placed over sand. If, after punching, there is a small dent in the sand under the area of a punch, then the martial artist has achieved some penetration power. Later, more cotton can be placed over the sand to improve penetration and impulse power.

Finally, to achieve accuracy the martial artist must first draw the figure of a man on a wall or sand bag with all the important cavities sketched in. In this book only 36 out of the 108 commonly attacked cavities will be listed. The particular 36 cavities are the ones more easily accessible to attack. (Some divisions emphasize particular cavities which may not be listed in this chapter.) After the figure is drawn in with appropriate locations for the cavities, the martial artist practices striking at the cavities until his accuracy and power are automatic and to the right depth.

With diligent practice, the martial artist can develop the advanced techniques of cavity press without necessarily developing internal power. But still, several years of practice are necessary. With cavity press Chin Na at his disposal, the martial artist has a technique which is the most admired in all Wu Su.

Striking Points of Cavity Press

Among the different styles in Chinese Wu Su, each style has its own special system of cavity press. Some styles emphasize certain hand forms, while others specialize in attacking a certain number or types of cavities. Even the name of the same cavity vary from style to style. In addition, although 108 cavities are available for martial purposes, no style will specialize in attacking every cavity. Even though each Kung Fu style emphasizes different cavities, the striking points of cavity press are the same 108 when taken as a whole.

In this book, out of the 108 cavities used in cavity press only 36 will be shown. Out of the 36, 24 are used for killing, 5 for paralysis, 5 for causing unconsciousness, and one for causing the loss of voice. The name of the cavity will be based on the ones given by acupuncturists. This will make for easy reference since the exact location of the cavities will not be given—a good book on acupuncture can be consulted for the exact location. In addition, the hand forms used to attack the cavities will be those that are most commonly used.

In addition to listing the 36 cavities with the attack forms, location, physical results, and cures for attacks, this section will contain a table which will show the relationship of the meridians and body areas to the time of attack. During every two hour period certain meridians and certain cavities on these meridians become more sensitive to strikes. During each time period three cavities become accessible to injury and attack; the techniques must therefore be coordinated with the time of day. Although three cavities become open to attack every time period, only one cavity will be listed.

1. Cavity Name: Baihui (fig. 164, A)
     Location: Top or crown of head
  Attack Forms: Palm
      Result: The bones of the head meet at this very sensitive spot. The power from an attack can easily penetrate into the soft brain matter. A powerful blow will literally smash the brain. This cavity is the point where the yin/yang change occurs. If the attack is moderate, dizziness and pain will occur.
   Meridian: Governing vessel (Related to cavity 23)
       Cure: If the attack is powerful, then the person will die—there is no cure. A moderate attack will require herbs.

2. Cavity Name: Shinchin or Yintang (fig. 164, B)
     Location: One half to one inch above eye bridge
  Attack Forms: Single Finger Fist, Double Finger Fist, Hammer Hand.
      Result: If attack is powerful, then death results because the brain and eyes are extensively damaged. A moderate attack will result in a swollen face.
   Meridian: Conception vessel
       Cure: If a heavy attack, there is no cure—damage is instantaneous. For a moderate attack, use massage and herbs; if not cured, the person can die from the internal bruise.

3. Cavity Name: Biliang or Meishin (fig. 164, C)
     Location: Eye bridge
  Attack Forms: Hammer Hand
      Result: Heavy attack leads to death because power will penetrate into brain. Moderate attack causes nose bleed.
   Meridian: Conception vessel
       Cure: Heavy attack has no cure. For a moderate attack stop the nose bleed.

4. Cavity Name: **Lianquan or Ienhou** (fig. 164, D)
    Location: Base of throat
  Attack Forms: Secret Sword, or choke by Eagle Claw, Dragon Claw, Tiger Claw, or Panther Claw
      Result: If attack is heavy, then death will result because heart will be affected. A moderate attack will cause the muscles and nerves to contract around the throat, thus resulting in unconsciousness.
   Meridian: Conception vessel
       Cure: No cure for heavy attack. For moderate attack, massage muscles and use herbs.

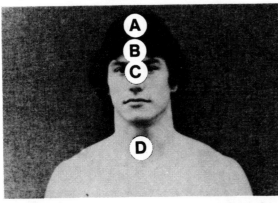

Figure 164

5. Cavity Name: **Taiyang** (left), **Taiyin** (right) (fig. 165, A)
    Location: Temple
  Attack Forms: Single Finger Fist, Double Finger Fist, Finger Tip
      Result: This cavity is the point of intersection for the gathering of the veins and arteries in the head. If the attack is powerful, the arteries will rupture, thus causing death. A powerful attack will also contract the nerves surrounding the head. If the attack is moderate, unconsciousness will occur.
   Meridian: Stomach
       Cure: No cure for heavy attack—ruptured arteries cannot be repaired. For a moderate attack, use massage and herbs.
6. Cavity Name: **Erhmen or Fontan or Xiaquan** (fig. 165, B)
    Location: Front of the ear
  Attack Forms: Single Finger Fist, Double Finger Fist, Finger Tip
      Result: The nerves to the head pass through this point before entering the temple. A heavy attack will contract the nerves going to the head and cause death. A moderate attack will produce unconsciousness.
   Meridian: Triple burner
       Cure: No cure for heavy attack. For a moderate attack, use massage and herbs.

7. Cavity Name: **Jiache or Yasha** (fig. 165, C)
    Location: Side of the jaw
Attack Forms: Single Finger Fist, Double Finger Fist, Finger Tip
      Result: Heavy attack leads to death; nerves at this point run into head. In a moderate attack the person will collapse and be unable to move.
  Meridian: Stomach
       Cure: No cure for heavy attack. For a moderate attack use massage and herbs.
8. Cavity Name: **Jugu** (fig. 165, D)
    Location: Top and middle of shoulder
Attack Forms: Grab with Eagle Claw, Tiger Claw, and Dragon Claw
      Result: Heavy attack will numb the shoulder.
  Meridian: Large intestine
       Cure: Massage

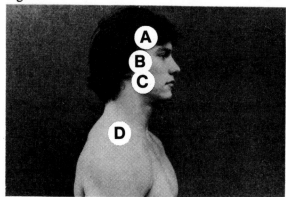

Figure 165

9. Cavity Name: **Binao** (fig. 166, A)
    Location: Outside of upper arm
Attack Forms: Eagle Claw, Tiger Claw, Dragon Claw, Panther Claw
      Result: Numbs arm
  Meridian: Large intestine
       Cure: Massage
10. Cavity Name: **Quchi** (fig. 166, B)
    Location: Front side of elbow joint
Attack Forms: Eagle Claw, Tiger Claw, Dragon Claw, Panther Claw, and White Crane Claw
      Result: Arm paralyzed
  Meridian: Large intestine
       Cure: Massage
11. Cavity Name: **Hegu or Fukou** (fig. 166, C)
    Location: Pit between forefinger and thumb
Attack Forms: Eagle Claw, Tiger Claw, Panther Claw, Dragon Claw, and White Crane Claw

Result: Heavy attack will affect heart, lung, and large intestine because the meridian passes these areas; death from organ failure will result.

Meridian: Large intestine

Cure: For a heavy attack, there is no cure. For a moderate attack, massage the whole arm.

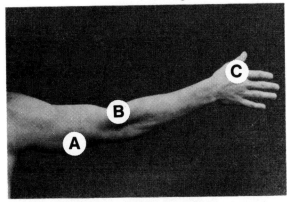

Figure 166

12. Cavity Name: Jiquan (fig. 167)

Location: Middle of armpit

Attack Forms: Secret Sword

Result: A heavy attack will result in a heart attack because this cavity lies on the heart meridian. A moderate attack will cause unconsciousness.

Meridian: Heart

Cure: No cure for a heavy attack. Massage and herbs for a moderate attack.

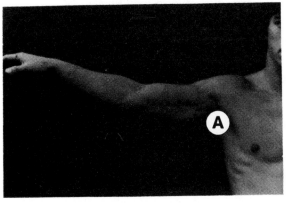

Figure 167

13. Cavity Name: Yingchuang or Giantai (fig. 168, A)

Location: Upper pectoral

Attack Forms: Single Finger Fist, Double Finger Fist, Secret Sword, and Palm

Result: The result of an attack on this cavity will depend on the side of the attack. If the left side Ying Chuang is attacked with power, then the heart will be damaged, resulting in death. A moderate attack to the left side will cause unconsciousness. A heavy attack to the right side will injure the nerves in the lungs—the person will continuously cough.

Meridian: Stomach

Cure: There is no cure for a heavy attack to the left side. For other situations use massage or strike the mirror cavity with a light force to release the pressure on the other side.

14. Cavity Name: Jiuwei or Hsinkan (fig. 168, B)

Location: Solar plexus

Attack Forms: Single Finger Fist, Double Finger Fist, Secret Sword, Palm, or any other form which has a pointed part.

Result: A heavy attack will cause death because the heart will be overwhelmed. A moderate attack will cause unconsciousness.

Meridian: Conception vessel

Cure: No cure for a heavy attack. For a moderate attack, strike the right lung to release pressure.

15. Cavity Name: Qimen (fig. 168, C)

Location: Base of rib

Attack Forms: Double Finger Fist, Palm, Single Finger Fist

Result: If the right side Chin Men is attacked with heavy power the liver will burst, thus resulting in death. Moderate force on the right side will cause unconsciousness. If the left side Chi Men is attacked, then the lung will be affected; a heavy attack will cause death and a moderate attack will cause coughing.

Meridian: Liver

Cure: No cure for heavy attacks. Massage and herbs for moderate attacks.

16. Cavity Name: Zhongwan (fig. 168, D)

Location: Upper stomach

Attack Forms: Fist, Palm, Kick

Result: A heavy attack will cause the inside organs to go into violent convulsions, thus causing death. A moderate attack will cause unconsciousness.

Meridian: Conception vessel

Cure: No cure for a heavy attack. Moderate attacks require massage and herbs to heal inside organs. Pinching on the back muscle will revive the victim.

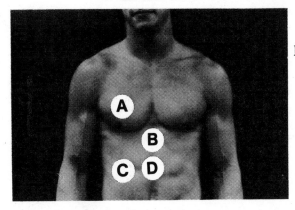

Figure 168

17. **Cavity Name: Zhangmen** (fig. 169, A)
    Location: Side of waist
    Attack Forms: Fist, Kick, Eagle Claw, Panther Claw, White Crane Claw, and Tiger Claw
    Result: Heavy attacks will cause the waist muscles to violently contract around the inside organs, thus causing death. Moderate attacks cause unconsciousness from pain and contractions.
    Meridian: Liver
    Cure: No cure for heavy attacks. For moderate attacks, massage chest and both sides of waist.
18. **Cavity Name: Neiquan or Wanmei** (fig. 169, B)
    Location: Inside of wrist
    Attack Forms: Eagle Claw, Dragon Claw, Tiger Claw, Panther Claw, and White Crane Claw
    Result: Heavy grasping can result in permanent injury to the inside organs. Person will have poor health. Person may faint.
    Meridian: Pericardium
    Cure: Massage whole arm and use herbs.
19. **Cavity Name: Qihai or Dantien** (fig. 169, C)
    Location: Slightly below belly button
    Attack Forms: Fist, Kick, Single Finger Fist
    Result: This cavity is the source of Chi. A heavy attack will prevent its movement, thus causing death. Moderate attacks will create a bruise.
    Meridian: Conception vessel
    Cure: For a heavy attack, there is no cure. Use herbs to cure bruise in a moderate attack.

20. Cavity Name: Shayin (fig. 169, D)

Location: Underneath groin

Attack Forms: Eagle Claw, White Crane Claw, Panther Claw, Tiger Claw, and Dragon Claw

Results: Heavy attack will cause death because there will be a violent contraction of the muscles in the groin area. In addition, this is the second cavity through which Chi will pass once it has left the Chi Hai cavity; this can make the internal organs lose their function. A moderate attack will cause unconsciousness.

Meridian: Liver

Cure: No cure for heavy attacks since damage is immediate. Massage and herbs are needed for moderate attacks.

Figure 169

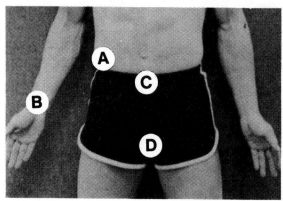

21. Cavity Name: Jimen or Baihai (fig. 170, A)

Location: Inside of thigh

Attack Forms: Eagle Claw, Tiger Claw, Panther Claw, White Crane Claw, Dragon Claw, and Kicking.

Results: Leg paralyzed.

Meridian: Spleen

Cure: Massage

22. Cavity Name: Taichong (fig. 170, B)

Location: Pit between first two big toes

Attack Forms: Kick by Heel, Eagle Claw, Tiger Claw, and Dragon Claw

Results: A heavy attack will cause unconsciousness. A moderate attack produces numbness of the foot.

130

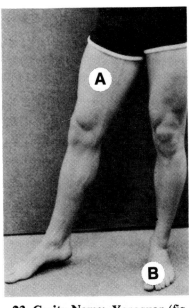

Figure 170

23. Cavity Name: Yongquan (fig. 171)
     Location: Bottom of foot
 Attack Forms: Eagle Claw, Dragon Claw, and Tiger Claw
      Results: Because this cavity is an important point on the kidney
               meridian, a heavy attack can cause death. A moderate
               attack will cause numbness.
     Meridian: Kidney
         Cure: No cure for heavy attacks. Massage for moderate at-
               tacks.

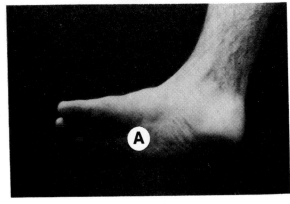

Figure 171

24. Cavity Name: **Yifeng or Tianzon** (fig. 172)

Location: Behind ear lobe

Results: A heavy attack will cause death because it will violently disrupt the nerves of the head. Moderate attacks produce unconsciousness.

Meridian: Triple burner

Cure: No cure for heavy attacks. Massage and herbs are needed for moderate attacks.

Figure 172

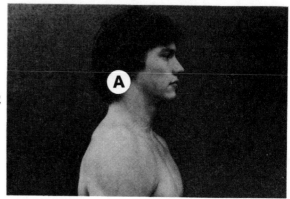

25. Cavity Name: **Yugen or Naohu** (fig. 173, A)

Location: Base of skull bone in back

Attack Forms: Hammer Hand, Fist, or Thumb Knuckle

Results: If power is heavy, attack will penetrate into the brain to cause death. A moderate attack will cause unconsciousness.

Meridian: Governing vessel

Cure: No cure for heavy attacks. Massage and herbs for moderate attacks.

26. Cavity Name: **Yamen** (fig. 173, B)

Location: Back of neck

Attack Forms: Secret Sword, Double Finger Fist, and Hand Knife

Results: Heavy attack will cause the person to lose his voice: nerves are connected to vocal cords from this spot. Moderate attack produces pain to neck or fainting.

Meridian: Governing vessel

Cure: Massage and herbs.

27. Cavity Name: **Tianzhu** (fig. 173, C)

Location: Back of neck

Attack Forms: Hand Knife

Results: Heavy attack results in brain damage and death. Moderate attack causes unconsciousness.

Meridian: Bladder

Cure: No cure for heavy attack. Massage and herbs for moderate attack.

28. Cavity Name: Jianjing (fig. 173, D)
      Location: Pit of shoulder
Attack Forms: Hand Knife, Double Finger Fist, Eagle Claw, Panther
              Claw, Tiger Claw, and Dragon Claw
      Results: Arms lose control if power is heavy
     Meridian: Gall bladder
        Cure: Massage

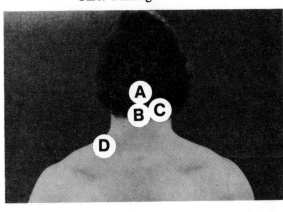

Figure 173

29. Cavity Name: Fengmen or Fonyen (fig. 174, A)
      Location: To the side of second vertebrae
Attack Forms: Secret Sword, Single Finger Fist, Double Finger Fist
      Results: If heavy power is applied, death will result. A moderate
              power will cause the lungs to contract, thus producing
              unconsciousness.
     Meridian: Bladder
        Cure: No cure for heavy attacks. Massage and herbs for mod-
              erate attacks.
30. Cavity Name: Dushu or Zudon (fig. 174, B)
      Location: Side of spinal cord
Attack Forms: Double Finger Fist
      Results: Heavy attack produces death. Moderate attack pro-
              duces unconsciousness.
     Meridian: Bladder
        Cure: For a heavy attack, quickly hit the chest to release
              power on back. For a moderate attack, massage and
              herbs.
31. Cavity Name: Lingtai or Baihsin (fig. 174, C)
      Location: Sixth vertebrae
Attack Forms: Fist, Single Finger Fist, Double Finger Fist
      Results: This cavity is the center of the nerves of the back. Also
              the heart is behind this cavity. Thus, a heavy attack will
              cause death. A moderate attack will cause vomiting of
              blood.

Meridian: Governing

Cure: No cure for heavy attacks. For moderate attacks, herbs must be used.

32. Cavity Name: Geguan or Fonwye (fig. 174, D)

Location: Under bottom of shoulder blade

Attack Forms: Fist, Palm, Single Finger Fist, Double Finger Fist

Results: A heavy attack will result in unconsciousness because the muscles will violently contract around the lungs. Moderate attack produces coughing or vomiting of blood.

Meridian: Bladder

Cure: Massage for both heavy and moderate attacks. Herbs are also required.

33. Cavity Name: Gienchu (fig. 174, E)

Location: Side of lower back

Attack Forms: Eagle Claw, Tiger Claw, Panther Claw, Fist, and Kick.

Results: If the right side Gien Chu is struck, then the liver is affected—thus a heavy attack will produce death. A heavy attack on the left side will rupture the spleen: if treated immediately, a heavy attack on the spleen can be remedied. Moderate attacks produce unconsciousness.

Cure: No cure for heavy attack on liver. Massage and herbs should be used for moderate attack.

34. Cavity Name: Jingmen or Hsiaoyao (fig. 174, F)

Location: Back of waist

Attack Forms: Palm, Fist, Eagle Claw, Tiger Claw, Panther Claw

Results: Heavy attacks will lead to death. Moderate attacks result in pain.

Meridian: Gall bladder

Cure: For heavy attacks there is no cure. For moderate attacks, massage and herbs must be used.

Figure 174

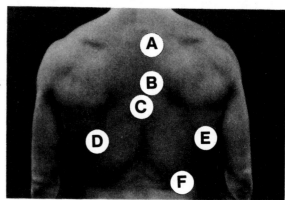

35. Cavity Name: Changqian or Wyelu (fig. 175, A)

Location: Tailbone

Attack Forms: Knee, Kick, Fist

Results: A heavy attack will result in death because the lower nervous system will have been destroyed. The person will not be able to defecate. A moderate strike will result in the person collapsing.

Meridian: Governing vessel

Cure: No cure for heavy attacks. Moderate attacks require massage and herbs.

36. Cavity Name: Weizhong (fig. 175, B)

Location: Middle of rear knee joint

Attack Forms: Eagle Claw, Panther Claw, Tiger Claw, Kick

Results: Leg paralyzed

Meridian: Bladder

Cure: Massage leg.

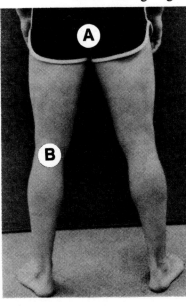

Figure 175

Treatment of Injuries from Advanced Chin Na

Any time a person becomes injured or is a victim of an advanced Chin Na technique (cavity press or sealing the breath or vein) immediate attention must be given to the person. Without immediate attention the person may, in a number of cases, die. The injuries that result from cavity press and sealing the breath or vein are much more serious in scope than the injuries that can result from the techniques of fundamental Chin Na.

When a person is made unconscious with a sealing the vein technique, it is vital to revive the victim before irreparable brain damage and death occur. In sealing the vein the closed arteries and veins sometimes will not open naturally by themselves. To open up the blood vessels it is necessary to strike the upper spine with the palm. By striking the upper spine the muscles on the side of the neck are forced to release their pressure on the arteries because the shock to the spine balances the original attack. The shock to the spine will tighten the muscles on the back of the neck; in turn, this will relax the muscle on the side of the neck. The strike to the spine must have the correct amount of power to balance the muscles; otherwise, too much power will add further injury, while too little power will have no effect. Another method of revival that some experienced martial artists use is to massage the affected area to reopen the arteries going into the brain.

The principle of balancing is also applied for reviving people who have been made unconscious by sealing the breath techniques. In sealing the breath, when a front chest cavity is attacked, it is necessary to hit the mirror-opposite cavity which is located on the back to balance the effects produced by striking the front of the chest. Striking the back cavity will release the violent muscular contractions of the chest. The location of the balancing cavities are not always in a symmetrical relationship to the original cavity. The martial artist must know those cavities before he can apply this remedy.

Almost the same method of treatment is used for people injuried by techniques from striking the Chi Chin Na. When a cavity is struck with enough power, a bruise will be created within its space. If the bruise was created from a strike that had internal power, then the bruise will stay deep in the cavity and cause adverse effects. If the bruise is in an extremely important cavity, the circulation of Chi can be stopped at that point, thus causing death. It is therefore important to get rid of the bruise within the cavity. Special herbs must be used to eliminate serious bruises in important cavities. These herbs are usually very potent in their ability to reach the cavity.

When a person is struck by the techniques of striking the blood, or if an internal organ is struck, there is no hope of recovery from a powerful and properly placed attack. No cure is available because the damage is immediate and instantly destructive to organs and blood vessels. This contrasts with a few types of striking the Chi where the adverse effects may take days to develop and show themselves. Because the damage to the organs and blood vessels are immediate and destructive, the victim will usually die.

CHAPTER 6

APPLICATION OF FUNDAMENTAL CHIN NA

The martial artist should realize that in Chapter 5 the fundamental techniques are essentially formulaic or dead until they can be applied in real situations. For example, almost every fundamental technique requires that the opponent touch the other person's body, but many of these techniques can be applied in practical situations without having the opponent grab first. By practicing the exact situations shown in Chapter 5, the martial artist becomes familiar and proficient in the use of the formula. The next stage is to discuss and practice with others the potential uses of the formula. There are almost a limitless number of situations in which the techniques can be applied—only at this stage do the Chin Na techniques become alive. The applicability of fundamental Chin Na is only limited by the research which the martial artist puts into it. This chapter, therefore, will show a few of the practical uses of Chin Na. In particular, the focus will be on the use of Chin Na for barehand versus barehand and barehand versus knife.

In terms of practical usage, one important point must be made. Although Chin Na is described as a seizing system, it can be used along with punches and kicks. Once an opponent is completely or partially controlled, the martial artist can easily find the simplest way to strike the controlled opponent, especially in the vital zones. Thus, even fundamental Chin Na can be used to kill. Sometimes certain opponents are too strong to be held by a Chin Na technique; the only alternative in these cases is to punch or kick vital zones.

Barehand vs. Barehand

To apply any Chin Na technique against an unarmed opponent requires the use of two principles. First, the martial artist should generally avoid using violent power against violent power. It is better to use or borrow the opponent's power against himself. Second, the execution of a Chin Na technique in a fighting situation requires that the legs, waist, and hands be finely coordinated. Chin Na techniques usually require more precision than other types of Wu Su forms.

A common technique used in most fights is the straight punch. There are many Chin Na techniques against a straight punch, but only two will be shown. As W punches in figure 1, B blocks from the inside with his right hand by using a White Crane Wing (see Chapter 3). Next, in figure 2, B's left hand slides under W's fist, taking hold of it. B then turns W's wrist clockwise while pulling it down and forward (fig. 3). Almost the same technique can be used by B if he blocks from the outside position as in figure 4. After blocking, B slides his left hand under W's wrist, grabs it, as in figure 5, and then turns the wrist counterclockwise, down and forward as in figure 6.

Figure 1

Figure 2

Figure 3

Figure 4

Figure 5

Figure 6

For a wide roundhouse punch, the kind of open punch an untrained person might throw, B first blocks up with his left hand as shown in figure 7. B quickly steps forward and locks his right hand under W's elbow. B then pushes forward with the left while jerking back with his right hand. B can then lock both of his hands over W's wrist (fig. 8).

Figure 7

Figure 8

Against an uppercut punch, B first blocks down with his left hand as in figure 9. B then grabs W's hand from the top (fig. 10), after which B immediately swings W's hand up clockwise using the method in figure 11. B's right hand twists W's wrist, while B's left helps in turning over the hands. B keeps turning while at the same time bending W's wrist in and also pushing down on W's forearm (fig. 12).

Figure 9

Figure 10

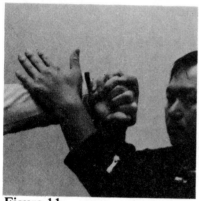

Figure 11

Figure 12

Another method against an uppercut is shown in figure 13 and 14. B blocks with his right hand and immediately slides it to the elbow while the left hand comes down on the wrist. When both hands are securely locked, B pulls with his right hand and pushes with his left.

Figure 13

Figure 14

Barehand vs. Knife

In any knife defense the first fact which will determine the defensive techniques is the way in which the opponent holds the knife. Basically, there are three ways that someone can hold a knife: these methods are shown in figures 15, 16 and 17. In the two overhand positions (fig. 15 and 16), the difference between them lies in which way the sharpened part of the knife faces. In figure 15 it faces inward while in figure 16 it faces outward. The positioning of the knife in figure 15 usually restricts the opponent to circular stabbing. The positioning of the knife in figure 16 allows for stabbing and slashing. On the other hand, the underhand grip in figure 17 allows for more versatility in stabbing and slashing—more angles of attack are available. The main disadvantage of the position in figure 17 is that stabbing must be done more or less on a straight path. The first two knife grips are for middle range attack while the last is for both long range and middle range attacks.

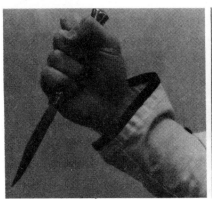
Figure 15

Figure 16

Figure 17

Before going on to the actual Chin Na techniques, there are some methods of knife defense for the martial artist who does not know, or who is not totally proficient in Chin Na. The first thing that a person can do is to wrap a piece of clothing around his hand and arm and use it for blocking (fig. 18). Once a block is made, B can kick. A second variation with the clothes is to hold the article taut and use it to deflect the knife attack as in figures 19 and 20. From these last two positions, it is not wise to wrap the article of clothing around the knife hand. To do so requires that the bottom hand pass in front of the knife—the opponent can easily stab the arm as it comes around. Another effective measure to use against a knife is to constantly snap one's belt at the face of the attacker (fig. 21). When an opening occurs, B can kick. Last, the martial artist can take off his shoes as in figure 22 and use them to block and strike. With all these methods the main purpose is to protect the hands against the knife and then to kick or punch when the opportunity arises.

Figure 18

Figure 19

Figure 20

Figure 21

Figure 22

Another important aspect in a knife defense is the necessity of not using violent power against violent power. The martial artist must follow the power of the opponent. Pitting power against power with an armed opponent is a fatal move. A small trained opponent with a knife is more than equal to a powerful man without a knife.

A third important aspect of knife defense is the necessity of using lateral movement. By moving sideways, attacks are easier to dodge and block. Usually, the most important first move in any Chin Na technique against the knife is moving laterally and blocking. Retreating straight back can at times be useful, but the maneuver is usually dangerous. It is always easier and faster for someone to move forward. Thus, an armed opponent can often catch up quickly to a retreating person.

Once the opponent's handling of the knife has been noted, the martial artist must use the appropriate blocking technique. Figure 23 shows the block to be used against an overhand stab; B would step to the side and catch W's hand from the outside while following W's power down. For an underhanded straight stab there are four methods of blocking. In figure 24 B blocks from the outside pushing the knife hand away. Figure 25 shows almost the same thing, but from an inside position: the hand is in a White

143

Crane Wing. The third method shown in figure 26 is to block by moving the hand up and to the outside of the wrist, thus making the knife hand slide to the side. The fourth block which is against a low stab (fig. 27) is done with the forearm. The forearm block can also be used from an inside position.

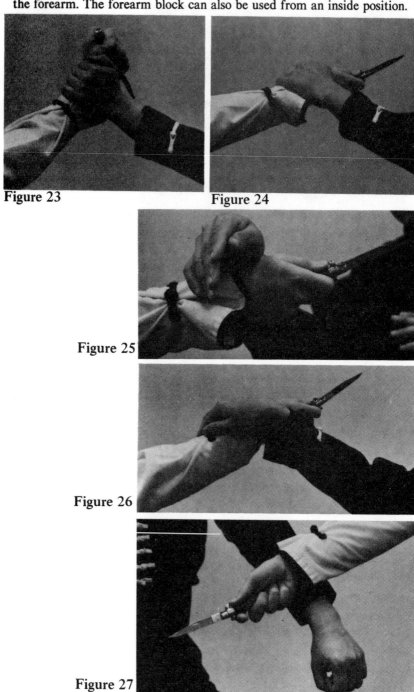

Figure 23

Figure 24

Figure 25

Figure 26

Figure 27

The first Chin Na technique against a knife attack (fig. 28), shows the beginning of a defense against the overhand stab with the sharp part of the knife facing inward. This technique may also be used with the sharp part facing out. As W attempts to stab from the top, B steps to the side and blocks as in figure 23. He then immediately slides his right hand up to grab W's wrist as in figure 28. Once the hand is secured, B turns the wrist counterclockwise, down and forward while pointing the knife towards W's face (fig. 29). If W struggles, B may force the knife into W. There are two basic variations to this particular Chin Na. First, as B turns W's wrist in figure 30, B may kick W in the groin as in figure 31. Second, when B has W's hand turned (fig. 32), B grabs W's hair while making sure not to let go of the knife hand. Next, B pulls W's head down and kicks him with the knee (fig. 33).

Figure 28

Figure 29

Figure 30

Figure 31

Figure 32

Figure 33

146

Next, figure 34 shows the beginning of an attack where W is holding the knife as in figure 16 while attempting to slash B from the side. B's first move is to step to the side and block as figure 34 indicates. B quickly slides his left, or minor hand, up to grab the knife hand. Then, B turns W's wrist clockwise, down and forward while bending B's hand into B's own wrist in figure 35.

Figure 34

Figure 35

Against the opponent who holds the knife as in figure 17, there are more techniques because the knife is in a more versatile position. In the start of the first technique (fig. 36), B blocks on the inside as W lunges forward to stab. B quickly slides his left hand under W's knife hand. With both hands, B turns W's wrist clockwise, down and forward while bending W's wrist (fig. 37). Figure 38 shows one variation of this technique; as B turns W's wrist, B kicks to the face.

Figure 36

Figure 37

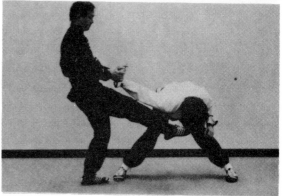

Figure 38

148

In the second technique against a straight stab, B blocks as in figure 36, but then simultaneously slides his right hand to the area above the elbow joint while the left hand grabs W's wrist; this action is shown in figure 39. B then jerks his own right hand down and in while pushing his own left hand forward (fig. 40). W's arm can be snapped out of joint if the jerking power is great.

Figure 39   Figure 40

The third technique against a forward stab begins with B blocking from the outside using the block in figure 24. B then slides his left hand to W's wrist and with both hands turns W's wrist counterclockwise (fig. 41). Next, B keeps hold of the knife hand with his left and pokes W in the eyes with his right hand (fig. 42). B may also kick the groin.

Figure 41   Figure 42

The fourth technique against a straight stab begins in figure 43 with the block on the inside. Once the block is made, B's right hand hooks under W's elbow (fig. 44). In figure 45, B simultaneously pushes down with his left hand while pulling in with the right; the whole arm is then locked at the elbow. In figure 45 W cannot stab because his elbow and wrist are locked. Figure 46 shows a variation of this technique. After the movement in figure 44, B pushes with his left hand and pulls with his right. B continues the motions until he can, as in figure 46, lock hands over W's wrist.

Figure 43

Figure 44

Figure 45

Figure 46

The last technique shows the use of the forearm for blocking a low stab. In figure 47, B blocks an attack with the left forearm while at the same time grabbing W's hand. B raises the arm and locks his left hand behind W's triceps while bending W's wrist (fig. 48). Then, as in figure 49, B pushes down on the wrist with his right hand and pulls with his left.

In all these techniques, it is important to practice them constantly with special emphasis on quickly observing the opponent's grip on the knife, lateral movement with blocks, and using the opponent's power against himself. Later, the martial artist can investigate the possibility of using other Chin Na techniques against various knife attacks. The formulas are ready at any moment to be made alive by the martial artist.

Figure 47

Figure 48

Figure 49

Conclusion

In using any fundamental Chin Na technique, whether for barehand against barehand or for knife against barehand attacks, there always exists some counterattack. The counterattacks are so numerous that they have not been shown. But during the practice of Chin Na techniques, an alert martial artist will be able to find the various counterattacks that exist. Once again, the research and practice that a martial artist puts into Chin Na will reflect his own ability in form and theory.

This particular chapter, while showing the practical applications of fundamental Chin Na, will not show the practical applications of the advanced Chin Na because such a subject is beyond the scope of this book. First, cavity press, which is considered the highest achievement among many Chinese martial artists, requires internal power, precise techniques, a good master to guide the student, knowledge of Chinese medicine, and years of martial experience. Once the martial artist has reached proficiency in cavity press, a process which alone takes ten or more years, the practical applications will be guided by his years of experience; a book, therefore, cannot hope to teach what only experience can teach. The same holds true for sealing the breath or vein.

In addition, only the professional martial artist who spends his life dedicated to Wu Su as an art and a moral path should attempt the mastery of cavity press. For the normal martial artist who has an outside career, the attempt to master cavity press will be nearly impossible because of outside concerns. For such martial artists, the fundamental techniques will be more than adequate for everyday martial purposes.

After reading this book, the martial artist will realize that the techniques of Shao Lin Chin Na encompass everything from the simple to the most complex. Among the fundamental techniques the martial artist will find many that are relatively easy to apply to everyday situations. The mastery of fundamental Chin Na is within the capacity of every martial artist regardless of style. With constant and diligent practice, the practitioner can find for himself useful techniques that help complement his system of martial arts.

Appendix 1

Table 1 — Time Table for Blood and Chi Circulation

CHINESE NAME FOR TIME PERIOD	TIME PERIOD OF 24-HOUR DAY	MERIDIAN	BODY AREA	CAVITY	CHAPTER & FIGURE NO.
Tzyy	23, 24, 1 (11:00, 12:00 pm, 1:00 am)	Gall bladder	Foot	Renzhong	Upper Lip
Choou	1, 2, 3 (1:00, 2:00, 3:00 am)	Liver	Waist	Biliang or Meishin	5-164, C
Yn	3, 4, 5 (3:00, 4:00, 5:00 am)	Lung	Eye	Baihui	5-164, A
Mao	5, 6, 7 (5:00, 6:00, 7:00 am)	Large intestine	Face	Jiache or Ya Sha	5-165, C
Chen	7, 8, 9 (7:00, 8:00, 9:00 am)	Stomach	Head	Taiyang	5-165, A
Syh	9, 10, 11 (9:00, 10:00, 11:00 am)	Spleen	Hand	Yingchuang or Giantai	5-168, A
Wuu	11, 12, 13 (11:00, 12:00 am, 1:00 pm)	Heart	Chest	Neiquan or Wanmei	5-169, B
Wey	13, 14, 15 (1:00, 2:00, 3:00 pm)	Small intestine	Stomach	Jiuwei or Hsinkan	5-168, B
Shen	15, 16, 17 (3:00, 4:00, 5:00 pm)	Bladder	Heart	Qihai or Dantien	5-169, C
Yeou	17, 18, 19 (5:00, 6:00, 7:00 pm)	Kidney	Back (Spleen)	Jimen or Baihai	5-170, A
Shiu	19, 20, 21 (7:00, 8:00, 9:00 pm)	Pericardium	Neck (Head)	Shayin	5-169, D
Hay	21, 22, 23 (9:00, 10:00, 11:00 pm)	Triple burner	Leg (Ankle)	Yongquan	5-171

Appendix 2

Translation of Chinese Terms.

阿達陀 A Da Taou
百把抓 Bai Bar Chuar
白海 Baihai
背心 Baihsin
百會 Baihui
八卦 Ba Kua
豹爪 Bao Chao
閉氣 Bih Chi
鼻樑 Biliang
臂儒 Binao
膀胱 *Bladder*
中央警官學校 *Central Police Academy*
採 Chai
長強 Changqian
長拳 Chang Chuan
張憲 Chang Shien
拆 Chei
辰 Chen
曾金灶 Cheng Gin Gsao
程學璨 Chen Shyue Shen
陳子正 Chen Tzu-Cheng
氣 Chi
劍訣 Chien Chueh

建國中學 *Chien Kuo Senior High School*
擒 Chin
秦檜 Chin Kua
擒拿 Chin Na
丑 Choou
周侗 Chou Ton
鍾手 Chuai Sou
任脈 *Conception vessel*
達磨 Da Mo
丹手 Dan Sou
丹田 Dantian
單指節 Dan Tzu Gieh
打 Dar
打血 Dar Shiee
蹬山步 Deng San Bu
习 Diao
轉化 *Dissolve by turning*
上化 *Dissolve up*
下化 *Dissolve down*
龍爪 Don Chao
坐盤步 Dsao Pan Bu
斷脈 Duann Mie
遁 Dun

督俞 Dushu
跌 Dye
耳門 Erhmen
方慧石 Fan Fai Shih
翻子 Fan Tzu
翻子鷹爪 Fan Tzu Ien Jao
法正 Far Cheng
飛 Fei
分筋 Fen Gin
順化 *Following the limb*
風門 Fongmen
洪堂 Fontan
鳳尾 Fonwye
鳳眼 Fonyen
夫 Fu
湖北省 Fu Bei
虎爪 Fu Chao
虎口 Fukuo
蓋 Gai
膽 *Gall bladder*
膈關 Gequan
將台 Giantai
精促 Gienchu
金 Gin Race
精忠報國 Ginn Chung Pau Kuo
金牌 Gin Pie
金紹峯 Gin Shao Fon
督脈 *Governing vessel*
龍大王 Great Dragon
工手 Gung Sou
韓琦 Han Chi
韓慶堂 Han Chin-Tan
亥 Hay
心 *Heart*

笑腰 Hsiaoyao
心坎 Hsinkan
形意 Hsing I
穴 Hsueh
鶴爪 Huo Chao
鶴翅 Huo Chiz
何鑄 Huo Juh
合谷 Hegu
河南省 Huo Nan Province
河北省 Huo Pei
易經 I Ching
咽喉 Ienhou
鷹爪 Ien Jao
顴 Jan
抓 Jaw
報 Jhan
轉 Jhuan
頰車 Jiache
肩井 Jianjing
箕門 Jimen
京門 Jingmen
極泉 Jiquan
鳩尾 Jiuwei
巨骨 Jugu
抓筋 Jua Jin
空軍幼年學校 *Junior Academy of the Chinese Air Force*
高濤 Kao Tao
靠 Kaw
腎 *Kidney*
扣 Kou
拐子馬 Kua Tzu Ma
功 Kung
功夫 Kung Fu

縱鶴拳 Tzon Huo Chuan
子 Tzyy
腕脈 Wanmei
委中 Weizhong
未 Wey
兀朮 Wuh Jwu
武當山 *Wu Dan Mountain*
午 Wuu
尾閭 Wyelu
啞門 Yamen
楊俊敏 Yang Jwing-Ming
牙腮 Yasha
躍 Yaw
揶 Yeh
黃河 *Yellow River*
酉 Yeou
岳飛 Yeuh Fei
岳武穆 Yeuh Wu Mu
岳雲 Yeuh Yun
醫鳳 Yifeng
易筋經 Yi Gin Ching
膺窗 Yingchuang
寅 Yn
岳家單 Yueh Jar Chun
岳家鷹爪 Yueh Jar Ien Jao
玉枕 Yugen
湧泉 Yongquan
雲南白藥 Yunnan Paiyao
扔 Zen
人中 Zenzhong
章門 Zhangmen
中脘 Zhongwan
啄 Zou
入洞 Zudon

Master Yang Jwing-Ming

ABOUT THE AUTHOR

Dr. Yang Jwing-Ming was born in Taiwan, Republic of China, in 1946. He started his Wu Su training at the age of fifteen under the White Crane (*Pai Huo* division) Master Cheng Gin-Gsao. Because White Crane is a Southern Division system emphasizing hand techniques and short and middle range fighting, Chin Na has become an important part of the style. Under Cheng Gin-Gsao, Dr. Yang mastered the White Crane system of Chin Na, along with mastering defense and attack techniques, massage, and herbal treatments. When Yang was sixteen (1962), he also began the study of Yang's Tai Chi Chuan with Master Kao Tao.

After graduating from high school, Yang went on to Tamkang College, Taipei, to study physics. While there, he began the study of Long Fist (*Chang Chuan*) with Master Li Mao-Ching at the Tamkang College Wu Su Club (1964–1968). Yang eventually became an assistant instructor under Li Mao-Ching. From Master Li Mao-Ching, Yang also learned the Eagle Claw (*Ien Jao*) method of Chin Na. Master Li Mao-Ching himself learned Eagle Claw Chin Na from his master, Han Ching-Tan. Han Ching-Tan learned Eagle Claw Chin Na as a second generation student of the Nan King Central Kuo Su Institute. Han Ching-Tan was a famous Chin Na instructor at the Central Police Academy, Taiwan, for over twenty years until his death in 1976.

While Dr. Yang was in Taipei, he continued his study of Tai Chi with several people. He has especially mastered the Tai Chi barehand sequence, pushing hands, the fighting sequence, the narrow blade sword, and the wide blade sword.

Yang has studied, practiced, and researched various systems of Chin Na from several masters and on his own. As a result, he has mixed and combined his knowledge of Chin Na into a system encompassing the White Crane and Eagle Claw methods.

In 1971 he completed his M.S. degree in physics at the National Taiwan University, and then served in the Chinese Air Force from 1971–1972. In the service, Yang taught physics at the Junior Academy of the Chinese Air Force while also teaching Wu Su. After being honorably discharged in 1972, he returned to Tamkang College to teach physics and resume study under Master Li Mao-Ching. Additionally, from 1968–1970 he taught Wu Su at Pan Chiao Senior High School and from 1968–1971 at the Chien Kuo Senior High School.

In 1974, Yang came to the United States to study mechanical engineering at Purdue University. Upon the request of a few students, he began to teach Kung Fu, with the result that the Purdue University Chinese Kung Fu Research Club was founded in the spring of 1975. While at Purdue, Yang also taught college credited courses of Tai Chi Chuan. In May, 1978, he was awarded a Ph.D. in mechanical engineering from Purdue.

In summary, Dr. Yang has been involved in Chinese Kung Fu (Wu Su) for eighteen years. During this time he has spent thirteen years learning Shao Lin White Crane (*Pai Huo*), Shao Lin Long Fist (*Chang Chuan*), and Tai Chi Chuan. Yang has twelve years of instructional experience: seven years in Taiwan and five years at Purdue University.

Master Cheng Gin-Gsao Master Li Mao-Ching